A NOVICE GUIDE TO

HOW TO
WRITE
A
THESIS

QUICK TIPS ON HOW TO FINISH
YOUR THESIS OR DISSERTATION

SHARAF MUTAHAR ALKIBSI

A Novice Guide to How to Write a Thesis / Sharaf M Alkibsi
Copyright © 2015 Sharaf M. Alkibsi
All rights reserved.

ISBN:1517741564
ISBN-13: 978-1517741563
First Edition: September 2015

10 9 8 7 6 5 4 3 2 1

DEDICATION

To students seeking to finish their degree

PREFACE

This book was written to help students start and finish their thesis or dissertation as part of their graduate program. The book is intended for students to read as they approach their thesis. It provides quick tips and advice about the research journey itself. It does not operate as a reference for research neither does it explains specific research techniques. It works along with your research manual or guidelines. It provides strategy, direction, hints, tips, warnings, cautions, and general advice related to the development of the thesis or dissertation.

This book is most useful to students looking forward to writing their thesis or dissertation. Advisors may recommend this book for their students at the early stage of their research project or if they struggle at any stage. The book addresses the big picture of the research journey, and provides advice on how to manage the entire process.

I have seen excellent students get stuck. All they needed to triumph was a piece of advice. I decided to write this book hoping to solve this problem for future students. Many small tips will be eye opening. A few tips will be mind blowing en route to scoring an outstanding thesis.

ACKNOWLEDGMENTS

Thanks to everyone who has participated in making this possible. My family, friends, and colleagues. I would like to credit these people for their contributions to this work.

Abdulkareem Al-Sayaghi
Adeeb Qassem
Adel Al-Huraibi
Adel Al-Mawri
Ahmed Al-Hadhrami
Ahmed Alkhauga
Ahmed Taqi
Ali Al-Ashwal
Amal Al-Kibsi
Ammar Aamer
Basem Al-Aghbari
Corey Arbor
Fadi Alaswadi
Hamoud Al-Najar
Harith Al-Hadrani
Janka Henami
Mary Lind
Maurice Shihadi
Mohammed Al-Abed
Mohammed Al-Aghbari
Mohammed Al-Awlaqi
Qusai Al-Muhatwari
Safa Al-Asbahi
Sinan Al-Marhadhi
Tarik Al-Sharafi
Waddah Othman
Waleed Al-Ward
Yusri Al-Baidhani

TABLE OF CONTENTS

INTRODUCTION

This book provides practical tips and guidelines helping Master's and Doctorate students start their thesis in order to reach a successful theory formulation. The book includes three main components you will need on your journey from beginning to end.

First, I'd like to discuss the thesis or dissertation, why it is necessary, and what it is expected to achieve. Then, I will discuss topic selection as the first challenge when writing a thesis, after which I will describe thesis content and the objectives of each component. This is to provide a clear, brief description of the thesis. I will also include different perspectives on where to start.

Second, I will look at the research journey, and what the journey includes with respect to your life, work, university program, and thesis stakeholders. I will address the relationship with your advisor, your committee members, and others. I will also address the journey tools that ensure you start your dissertation knowing what is coming up.

Third, I will address your theory. I will look closely at each of your thesis components in detail and provide you with important tips and hints to nail it down. I will go into detail on each milestone and provide examples of best practices, including the dos and don'ts.

This book is recommended for students at the early stages of thesis development. It is not intended as a step-by-step manual for the thesis process, but rather providing an important thesis development roadmap.

CHAPTER 1: THE THESIS

Why a Thesis?

Why do students have to write a thesis? First, it is a requirement for your program to earn a degree. A thesis or a dissertation is usually evidence that the student has accumulated experience in conducting research. This requirement provides evidence that the student can graduate. It proves that the student is capable of doing research, identifying a problem, building models, investigating literature, making use of available research methods, knowing the differences in research methods, collecting data, then coming up with conclusions. The thesis provides a comprehensive exercise that once the student has passed, he or she has gone through many problem-solving challenges that involve knowledge building, and truth finding.[1]

Throughout the book, I will refer to your project as a thesis or dissertation. In the context of this book, they mean the same thing. Different programs may have different objectives that will be discussed later in this book.

What does the thesis or dissertation try to achieve? The thesis or dissertation tries to find the truth about a topic. The researcher tries to gather all available data, research, and findings to reach a conclusion. This truth-finding mission is important to develop learning and to gain insights into a specific topic. As students proceed through the process, they gain experience and apply existing knowledge to solve a new problem, to understand new phenomena, or to provide a new interpretation of a given topic. This process is described here as a journey of finding the truth. As you take the journey, you need to provide evidence that you have gone through the journey successfully, meaning that you can take this journey again on your own and achieve reliable results that create new knowledge or trends in the field of study.

The important part of the dissertation objective is you. You are the key component. It is important that you take the journey with your advisor's help. Your program may call your advisor as your mentor, committee chairperson, or supervisor. As you take the journey, you start to learn the process on how to find the truth, and learn techniques that will guide you on how to achieve it independently next time.

Your success in the journey is measured by how well you make use of the techniques to achieve your research objective. Your research objective is just an example of any research objective that you may want to explore in the future. However, it is not important by itself; you are the most important factor in the entire exercise. The research is just a means to ensure you can do the exercise.

Taking the truth-finding journey is similar to the challenge of learning to drive a car. First, you need to learn how to drive well. Then, you need to get a driver's license. During the driver's license test, you have to show you can operate a car. It does not matter what car you drive, but what is important is that you demonstrate driving skill. Some may drive a car with an automatic transmission, others a standard transmission. The type of the car does not matter. What matters is that the driver knows effective driving techniques.

When you do a driving test, you may have to demonstrate your capability by driving a short distance. You have to turn on the engine, accelerate, move, and reach a destination. This is similar to your thesis journey.

Sometimes the examiner may ask you to do certain moves to prove that you know a wide variety of driving techniques. These moves are tested during the thesis oral defense or the Viva. The Viva is the British equivalent of an oral defense.

The purpose of the driving test is not for you to reach an important destination, such as your office or a hospital. Likewise, the purpose of a thesis is not to reach a conclusion or an important finding. However, if you actually reach an important conclusion, that is great, and you should attempt to publish a journal article from your thesis (during or after graduation). Published theses carry more credibility in the academic community. Therefore, the actual findings are only important after you pass and receive your license or degree.

In summary, the thesis is a truth-finding journey. It provides evidence that you, the student, are familiar with the different research techniques and are able to use them. The thesis is evidence you are a master or a doctor of a particular subject.

A Thesis Example

You lost your keys. That is your problem statement. The objective now is to find your keys. The research question is "Where are my keys?" Your hypothesis is "My keys are in my office because that was the last place I remember having them." Another hypothesis may say, "My secretary may know where my keys are because she saw me holding them when I stepped into the office."

Your research methodology may include a qualitative research method which relies on interviews, such as asking your secretary where your keys are. Alternatively, your research may be quantitative which relies on investigating references, such as whether the keys are in a particular location.

In the end, you may or may not actually find your keys. It does not matter. What matters is that you tried your best to find them. At least, this is what you would expect from your children before trusting them with your keys.

This simple example demonstrates the research process. What is important is that you document what you did; provide an answer (positive or negative) to the research question; and conduct the research logically. It is important that you keep your eyes open in the search process, listen carefully, keep your objective in mind, and do the search thoroughly. After you understand the findings, make them productive, document them, and then reach a conclusion.

In this example, the conclusion would be the answer to "Where are my keys?" which is the research question. You may have additional conclusions, like "Secretaries may be a good source of information when searching for keys." which may be published as well so next time someone searching for keys might try this methodology.

If you happen to have read this research, you may create a new research topic that would ask many questions because of those new findings. You may ask for example "Where are keys mostly found when lost?" This new research may replicate some of the previous studies, or follow its logic, develop its methodology, provide a new way to address the problem, and a wide range of development to improve our understanding of handling lost keys and to enrich knowledge on how to solve similar problems.

Choosing your topic

So where do you start with your topic? There are many ways to come up with a topic. For example, you may want to start to look back at your school subjects and remember the topics you enjoyed. What theories did you find interesting? Which instructor inspired you? What lesson did you find fascinating and desired to study more?

You may also want to think about your job. What do you do that is covered in the literature? What topics have experts in your field worked on? What problem at your job was worth researching and studying?

Another area by which you can search for a topic is by reading journal articles. Check the "further research" section of the articles that you read. If you choose to pursue some of the "further research" suggestions, make sure you are reading up-to-date articles, a maximum of two years old.

This can be time-consuming, but it works if you are stuck. If you decide to take this route, be careful of falling into a state of not having a topic for too long. This exercise needs to be short.

Finding a topic can be a nightmare because some students, if they do not land on their topic fast enough, are never satisfied with any topic. Even if later they decided on a topic, they still remember the reasons that kept them without a topic for a long time. Therefore, do not let this issue overwhelm you.

You need to find a topic very quickly and early in the process. If you do not have a topic, many times, you may also not find an advisor. Many advisors need to know the topic before they agree to work with you. Advisors generally prefer to work with a topic that aligns with his or her research interests. Alternatively, you may find an advisor who already has a topic for you that may also interest you.

Finding the topic that your advisor prefers can help you with your degree, and this puts more pressure on the advisor to help you. The advisor will be very detailed on what is required and how it should be conducted. This can be demanding, but it is great for the final product. You may fall in conflict with the advisor on issues in which you have different takes if you do not have ground rules and mutual expectations agreed upon. A debate can be very enlightening. The least advantageous point in this regard is that you may be conducting a study about which you are not very 'passionate.' This is OK. Again, the thesis or dissertation is a journey and students just need to go through it.

Passionate ideas

"Choose a subject about which you are passionate," is very common advice when it comes to thesis topics. Many relate it to the questions of what field of study you want to study after you graduate from high school. However, this is a bit different. Remember your research topic in your thesis is choosing an example topic to demonstrate your abilities to conduct research. At the same time, the journey will take some time, from six months to a few years. You might as well make good use of your time on a topic you enjoy. Remember, that by the end of your journey, you will be an expert in your subject and have read much of its literature.

You may want to consider a topic related to your job. This can provide you with in-depth experience that can develop your career further. It can also give you the chance to read all the books you always wanted to read for work. Nevertheless, be careful because it is not always like that.

When selecting a topic related directly to your work, it is not exactly your work. Remember, this is an exercise journey with an objective to prove your ability to research, not your ability to do a job. Unless your work is academic research, then it will probably be a different focus.

A student of mine used to work as a procurement officer for an international NGO. He decided to write a thesis on how bad the current procurement process is at his work. I am sure you can imagine the consequences of this route. You may not know it easily, but eventually; you may find yourself in this situation.

The problem with working on a thesis that is highly linked to your work is that you may be passionate about not only the topic, but also about how the data should look, and how the findings need to turn out. Also, you need to be prepared to defend your thesis in front of your boss without having a conflict of interest situation.

You do not want to reach conclusions that you deeply believe to be true while the data or research findings prove otherwise. Reaching such situation will make the journey achieve an objective other than its original objective. It also starts to generate conflicting goals and views between what you should be doing, and what you should be concluding. A very dangerous route one may fall in is to manipulating, fabricating, or misinterpreting the data.

If you choose a topic related to your field of study, try to keep the questions to those about which you truly want answers. Do not jump into what the findings should or may tell, rather keep it as a question that you are interested in understanding rather than a conclusion you want to prove.

My student at the NGO decided to take this route: what factors make up an effective NGO? He was interested in finding out what answers might come, and he did not have anything in mind to prove or disprove ahead of the research process.

The findings of the study can help you spend some good time in your work topics. They can also provide you with insightful information and research that can help you shape your overall understanding of your field. Try to make the findings interesting to most of your colleagues and coworkers. This will provide you with in-depth general expertise in your area of study.

Narrow it down

Now that you have selected your topic, narrowing it down should not take you back to change your topic. Sometimes it does, but you really should not have to. If you feel you have to change your topic, then you may need help finding the best route in narrowing it down.

Narrowing your topic is all about choosing the angle you will take in your study. There are some classic approaches you can find in the literature. One way is to go to the library and start reading what other articles talk about under your topic. This is a very good route, as it will keep your study current, and related to what everyone else in your topic is researching.

When you go to the library, whether physical or online, try to find some interesting papers that are related to what you want to do. An excellent research topic occurs when you build your study on someone else's findings.

For example, let us say your topic is mobile telecommunication. You research the topic and find an article that provides information on how customers are satisfied with mobile telecommunication companies when provided with loyalty points. You can test this theory in your study.

When having another paper, thesis, or research as your model and you start following the previous researcher's theory or findings, you have a clear roadmap for your study. Just like when you drive behind another car to make sure that your speed limit is relatively correct, or you follow a navigation system in your driving journey.

There is nothing wrong in replicating a study to check it or validate it. In fact, many times, your replication can be very important for you to achieve your research exercise, and for the original author who will have you to validate or challenge his or her findings.

Keep it simple

Keeping the topic simple is important because the topic is not the challenge rather a journey itself. So do not over burn yourself in selecting the topic or narrowing it down because that is not the challenge. Besides, your advisor or school requirements should help you choose your topic, and your responsibility is to make it simple and proceed. What will stick with you is your research journey and how you did it. Nevertheless, the topic will only prove that you can do it once. Then in the future, you can do more research on other topics that you wish to tackle effectively.

Nobel Prize

Sometimes, while you are thinking about your degree and your thesis, you start to think this is your chance to prove to the world a new theory. Some people believe this is their chance to get a Nobel Prize. However, the truth of the matter is that it is not the time for this daydream.[2]

Your research thesis or dissertation is not meant for you to get world attention. It is an item on your degree checklist. This checklist has an item that says the student can research in this field of study. Nothing more, nothing less.

While some people earn Nobel Prize afterward, it is because they had been able to do what they had to do when they had to do it. So let the Nobel Prize be your objective to start looking for later. Only after you finish this task, think of the Nobel Prize.

Having said this, it does not mean that your thesis or dissertation cannot help you get closer to the Nobel Prize. It can help you; it is just not the objective. So how can your thesis help you get closer to the Nobel Prize? For example, Jean Tirole wrote his thesis on economic theory in the year 1981. He continued his work and in 2014 won the Nobel Prize for economics.

When you select your topic, and as you narrow it down, you may want to do a good survey of the current literature and understand the hot topics that are mainly discussed. What did Nobel Prize winners do in the past to earn such prizes? You may want to look at who are famous or current authority researchers in your topic field that said anything about what.

Last year, I decided to conduct a seminar at my university titled, "Current Research Needs By Industry Professionals." Guests invited were leaders in their fields who shared with graduate students topics needing to be researched now. This provided an excellent start for many students to think about what to research as indicated by experts.

Every journal article in your peer-reviewed database has a recommendation for future research. Editors of academic journals call for papers about specific topics. They truly mean that you are requested to think about researching just this. In fact, if you contact these researchers and editors, they may provide you with the path to a Nobel Prize.

Overview of Your Thesis

Now that you have selected your topic and narrowed it down, you normally need to start Chapter 1. There are usually five chapters in most programs and very few programs have different layouts. Here, I will describe each chapter for you to get an understanding of the chapters. It will include what each chapter entails, before discussing the actual writing process.

Understanding what each chapter does in your thesis and what exactly it includes is important for you to understand even before selecting your topic. Therefore, I am not surprised you are reading this before even choosing your topic. If you have already selected your topic, keep in mind that you may really want to change your topic after reaching this entire section of chapter descriptions because you now will know what it means to do a thesis or a dissertation.

You may want to go to a restaurant to eat, but after realizing how many bus changes are needed to reach it, you can easily change the venue and eat elsewhere.

Thesis Chapter 1: Introduction (Your Theory)

This chapter includes your theory. What do I mean by a theory? I mean your very specific topic; your exact research idea or hypothesis. Your theory is the final conclusion of your study. An example of theory would be "ABC types of keys are less likely to be lost than XYZ keys" given the earlier lost keys example.

Your first chapter may start with the introduction, background information, your problem statement, a research purpose or objective, a research question, a hypothesis, the conceptual or theoretical framework, the importance of your research, its relevance to knowledge and industry, and your plan of study.

The following sections will discuss each of the components per many programs. These are provided as guidance, but it is important that you follow your program's specific guidelines.

Thesis Chapter 2: Literature Review

This chapter focuses on what others in the field have said about your topic. Here you will document important research relative to your study. It does not include everything you have read about your topic. Rather, it will only include relevant literature that is important for the reader to understand your research.

A literature review shows that you, the researcher, have done your homework. What was your homework? It was to see what has been researched about your topic or theory. What did previous researchers say about your research question? What did the "older" or "more experienced" people do to tackle your problem, or answer your questions? Were there any specific recipes to solving similar problems? Were there any models that addressed your topic that can be used to answer your research questions?[4]

If there are any controversies regarding your topic, this might be a good point to address the controversy and choose one side or the other. You are providing the reader with the background information needed to understand the topic.

In Chapter 2, you are requested to go to the library and read about the topic, the problem, the research question, your hypothesis, and report them. This means that you will read many papers, and only bring the important ones to your study.

Going back to the "lost keys" example, you may start searching for the concept of lost keys; why people lose them, what factors make people lose keys, and what factors help people remember their keys' location. You may find literature that discusses short-term and long-term memory. You may find a study that asserts people around you might trigger one's short-term memory. In other words, asking the secretary about your keys may help you remember where you lost them given her attempt to answer your question.

If we did not do the literature review, it would be like trying to fix your car without checking a repair manual. The literature review will help you to organize your research and provide you with the method, model, roadmap, tools, surveys, interview questions, data, and other information.

Besides, the literature review will give you the knowledge of what others have been doing in this field, so you may want to learn from them, and make use of their experience. In the end, an important part of your degree is your ability to learn from others and build on their conclusions. If you do not do it well, you may struggle to find lost keys or to solve your research problem properly.

From a journey perspective, if you do not do a good literature review, you will not be an expert on your subject matter. You may not sound like someone who really did full coverage of the study. Remember, when you go to visit a city and you do not see everything in it, or miss the important monuments that distinguish that city, you cannot prove to have visited it. Imagine you visited Egypt, and never saw the pyramids.

Thesis Chapter 3: Methodology

This chapter explains your research methodology. What did you do to obtain your information? Did you use a survey or did you conduct an interview? Did you experiment or did you observe? How did you collect your data? With whom did you talk? How did you select them? Was that a proper or reasonable method to collect the information?[5]

You will address your unique data collection method in this chapter. It will describe your research methodology. For example, was it quantitative or qualitative? Did you develop a survey , or did you use someone else's survey? Did you do a pilot study? Do you have any specific approach to data analysis?

This chapter may require you to get assistance from your advisor to make sure you are using a proper method. There are countless methods that can lead you to Rome. Each method has its advantages and disadvantages. Some may involve special arrangement. Each has its limitations and opportunities. Specific methods may direct your research findings towards a different direction. Every method has its own set of tools and techniques to proceed to the following chapters. Different methods may mean different conclusions.

You will probably need to look up your specific methodology. For example, if you decide to do an online survey , you will probably need to learn how to make online surveys and the techniques associated with them. In this book, I try to address some of the common methods such as surveys, but you may want to get a specialized book on your analysis methodology.

Your methodology will dictate the type of analysis that you will have to do in Chapter 4. This is very normal. It should not scare you to the point you change it. In fact, all methods will take you to the following analysis step in Chapter 4.

Thesis Chapter 4: Findings

In this chapter, you will list the findings of your research methodology. You will describe your findings, analyze them, and interpret them to your readers. For example, if you have decided to do a survey, here you will report who filled the survey, what they said, and what that says about your research question.[6]

This chapter lists all findings answering your research questions. They will describe the answers you went for in your research questions. It will include all the graphs, comments, observations, experiment test results, and their analysis. These findings will show if your findings agree or disagree with previous research or literature discussed in Chapter 2.

Reaching this section indicates you have finished your research. Now is the time to write it down, and make it understandable to everyone else. As you write this section, you probably know the results of your study, and you have reached the truth about your topic.

In Chapter 4, you tell your readers what you have discovered. This chapter will say where your "lost key" was found. It will discuss how the methodology was successful in reaching the lost key. This chapter is also the one that will say, "We did not find the key" even though we have conducted the methodology correctly. This chapter may provide information about possible flaws in the questions, participants of the study, representation of the sample, and many other contributing factors to the findings.

Thesis Chapter 5: Conclusion

Chapter 5 is the last chapter. It presents the conclusions and recommendations. It provides the result of the study and answers the problem statement. It discusses lessons learned from the research study. It will provide a link between the findings in Chapter 4 and the literature in Chapter 2. It will discuss how each finding in Chapter 4 answers the research questions in Chapter 1. It will address any surprising findings in Chapter 4. [3]

If you did not find the "lost key," Chapter 5 should indicate what could have gone wrong in the research process. It may advise future researchers of their lost keys to investigate new or different locations. It will provide the reasons the keys were not found. It can also provide advice on how not to lose the key in the first place. Many conclusions can be possible at the end of the research.

Chapter 5 should follow a clear logical link all the chapters. It needs to draw a conclusion based on what was discovered in Chapter 4, with what was mentioned in Chapter 2, given the methodology chosen in Chapter 3, and to address the theory in Chapter 1. This important relationship is crucial for you to understand and to see how the big picture of your thesis is formed. If you decide to modify your Chapter 5, pay attention to the fact that you will need to modify other chapters to reflect such change. Every chapter is a building block of the entire thesis that needs to be consistent and coherent. The entire study needs to be harmonious.

Chapter 5 includes your final wisdom and your recommendations for your research. After you finish your thesis, you may be requested to defend it or to present it. While the previous four chapters are important to demonstrate to your committee, Chapter 5 takes it to the next step in your endeavor. People who cite your work would say that you concluded, "Lost keys are always found with the help of secretaries."

Starting the Study

Think of your research study as a journey searching for gold. You are now the researcher who wants to find gold, which is the truth about a specific topic. When you search for gold, you have a few milestones that you have to achieve. You will have to check with the previous literature of where gold is. Maybe check a map of hidden treasures. You may want to see what previous researchers have done. You want to cite everyone who has searched for the same gold and provided valuable findings to help you find it. These citations are your literature review.

Once you have learned from the literature that your gold lies in a particular place, then you will need to get the tools necessary to find it. You will need to establish a methodology that is going to be your primary tool in finding the truth about the universe. The tools used to get gold may include a metal detector that will beep every time gold is near. This tool may be helpful especially when you know that gold tends to be close to other metals as explained by the literature review.

Another methodology to find gold is to ask the proper people who live or operate in the geographical place you are investigating. Questions that are relevant to gold finding, such as "have you heard of the availability of gold in this area?" This can be an example of how interviews work. You are trying to explore the area, and you may want to gather the opinions of people around that area. Now, their opinions may not matter. You may already know that they do not know the answers. If they did know, they might have already found it. In our context, papers must have been written about it already.

Regarding the previous discussion, I would like to point out two important issues in research. One, you need to have good logic to determine what you will do to find the gold, and use the proper method to reach it. Sometimes, one can focus too much on the trees to the point you cannot see the forest.

Another example of what your research study journey looks like is traveling from one place to another. Let us say that you want to go to a place you have never been. You will need to research this just as you research your thesis.

You need to decide where you will go. Then you need to discover the place while there. You may want to spend a month on vacation, but you have to make that decision, and you have to stick to it. During this journey, you need to get the most out of it. You want to be able to make full use of your time to get the best memories out of this vacation. In our context, you want it to produce the most learning possible.

Your literature review of this vacation may include quick online surfing about your destination. You may decide to visit more in-depth sites about specific places to plan your vacation better. The more time you spend searching, the more enlightening your vacation will probably be. You may talk to people who have been there, and get their advice on what to do and where to go. Nevertheless, nothing is close to what you can find online, especially if you find the right website that includes details about your destination.

You will then need to compile vacation details, such as the method that makes your vacation a rich experience. You will need to reserve hotels, book flights, and identify the locations you want to visit. This is a plan of action that will generate your vacation findings. A proper plan will make a great vacation. A poor plan will probably waste your month of vacation.

Do you remember a good vacation you had? Do you remember a poor vacation you had? The reasons those vacations were good or bad will likely make your thesis or dissertation journey successful or not very successful. I advise you take some time to think about this analogy.

You, the researcher or the vacationer, are the unit of implementing, planning, finding, and concluding the research, or the vacation. Selecting the right destination is important. Selecting the right companions is a key. Methods used for transportation, touring, and sightseeing are critical. Making use of available resources is a personal approach to your journey.

Above, I discussed two examples. One is the search for gold and the second is the search for a rich vacation. These two examples have a fundamental difference. In the first example, you know where you have to achieve your goal. You know its value, and everyone else knows its value. In the second example you are enjoying a journey and you know its value. However, others may not. The gold journey is more focused and determined to produce a solid conclusion that is well defined. The vacation journey is more flexible and creative. Both can generate important findings. The message here is that you need to know whether you are taking a focused and determined journey or a flexible and creative one. The following discussion should be an eye opener to the big picture.

Looking at the Big Picture

Before you start your thesis, you need to look at the big picture. After you have an idea about the thesis chapters and content, you need to start thinking about the journey from start to end. Sometimes, if you go to a new place, you can just hit the road, and then solve problems as you go. Another way to take a journey is by examining the entire trip before starting. For example, you need to make sure you know where you can eat, sleep, fuel, and rest.

In the following sections, I will try to give you hints on where to start your research journey. While many would follow the classic chapter sequence (one, two, three, four, etc.). Here I will give you different routes to finishing your thesis. The key hint is not starting from Chapter 4, because you actually cannot. However, let us start thinking about your research from Chapter 4. The reason one may want to start from the different chapters is to think about specific milestones that one will have to face along the journey.

Start from Previous Research– Ch. 2

Your research journey can start from Chapter 2. Chapter 2 is the literature review chapter. So you start your journey by reading the literature. The more you read, the more you narrow your topic. And as you read from different journals, the more you learn about current research trends. This will give you an insight into your research journey. It will help you decide where and how to get going.

Reading the literature will provide a big shift in your research idea. You can search "Google Scholar" and see what research articles are there and what they discuss. Searching in your topic domain will provide you with a list of journals and authors who are discussing issues related to what you may be interested in doing.

The best way to start your thesis is when you build on the current literature. The best thesis you can make would say something like the following:

> Research conducted by John last year indicated that future research might want to measure the impact of X on Y. This research study will just do that.

Here's another way:

> Research conducted by Adam two years ago measured the impact of X on Y. This study will validate Adam's finding in a different setting.

A third way:

> Research conducted by Smith last year found five important issues to affect X. This study will examine these five issues.

A fourth way:

> Research conducted by Sam this year indicated X and Y. This study will explore X.

The common theme among the above examples is that you are taking a piece of literature that is suggesting a research question for you. If you search within that research question, you may find others who have already started researching in the same area. Also, if you contact the author, he or she may already be working on answering this suggested research question. As you dig more into the area, you will learn more information about the possible research questions and topics in a more specific manner.

The power of this route is that you become an expert as you read more of current research on a specific topic. This topic may have never been in your mind, and as you normally search, your eye would not catch the importance of the topic just because you were ignorant about it.

When finding this piece of literature, it is preferable to have been published within the past five years. Literature published earlier than that begs the question: if no one else has thought of studying it, why you? In such a case, you will need to do another literature review to answer why others have not answered it and make your case. The chances are researchers may already have addressed that topic and new questions have already emerged. Therefore, keep searching and you will find the updates in this research field and pick a newer study.

A good start in your thesis is to have one to three journal articles that you consider the core of your study. Let us call these journal articles your Model Journal Articles. Whether you start from Chapter 2 or you start from another chapter, you will ultimately need to have one or more journal articles as your study base.

It is important to understand this journal article, its full meaning, its basis, and its findings and conclusions. This will help you build a strong thesis and limit the amount of literature you will need to research.

For example, if you find a good journal article that covers the essence of your study. This journal article will include a literature review. This literature review will be similar to your literature review. It does not mean that you will copy and paste; rather it means that you know where to read more about the topic.

Looking at the references list of your model journal article will limit your research needs; you will just need to look up these references and understand their contribution to your field of study. Besides, this journal article will briefly describe concepts, allowing you to identify important and less important references for your research objective.

It is important that you find good journal articles from reputable journals to get quality results. If you build your article on a poor article, you will inherit that limitation. You will need to find another journal article and follow its references.

A great thing about technology is the ability to find journal articles. Previous books on research would spend a few chapters on how to deal with the library, but nowadays, technology has significantly eased this process. I will discuss this later in this book.

In this context, the relevance of technology is that you can see if a journal article has been cited by others, and how many other studies cite it. This will give you an indication of how relevant and critical the content of your model journal article is.

You may have more than one journal article that act as models. You may have a journal article for your research questions. Another one is for your methodology. A third one is for your statistical analysis. This way, you do not get lost in how to analyze a specific method, or how to conclude based on a specific type of analysis. You can just understand the method used in that model, and replicate it.

Start with the Methodology – Ch. 3

Sometimes it is very easy to start with your Chapter 3 before you get into anything else in your thesis. When I say, "..anything else in your thesis," I mean you have a topic but have not developed anything in Chapter 1, such as a research question. Maybe you have already started your program, and you have some knowledge about your field of study, but have not yet decided on the title for your thesis.

A good start is to ask yourself what kind of research do you want to do? Do you want to do a survey, an interview, observations, an experiment, or a case study? Starting here may help get your thesis off the ground quickly.

Psychographic studies divide people into achievers, dreamers, makers, and others. Makers are those who want to start the execution immediately. You may have an immense preference for an execution method that gives you an advantage and leverage if you start from the methodology.

Starting from the methodology will help you narrow your research for ideas, problems, types of research questions, hypothesis, and focus. The methodology is the tool used in your study to achieve your conclusion. So one may wonder how that can be a starting point.

Consider this example; you really want to do a survey. You believe that you are good in quantitative analysis, and therefore, you want to do a correlation study. This narrows down your topic and gives you a limited number of research areas and research questions to ask. Now your research question would be more of checking, measuring, examining, and counting type of questions. You are probably going to use Excel or SPSS to analyze your data. You would probably be talking about significant difference and statistical methods of measurements.

On the other hand, let us say you prefer a qualitative approach. Researching via an interview method would mean a few visits to key stakeholders asking them questions regarding a particular topic. This can be an appealing research method that you want to do in your thesis regardless of everything else.

If you take the interview route, then your research question would be what, why, and how types of questions. You would be exploring in your questions and hoping to find the truth from a conversation rather than a validation of any information. Your questions would be looking for answers that you do not know, and that the literature does not fully cover.

Your final findings would be recorded interviews, notes, transcriptions, and statements. Then, you will analyze patterns, common ideas, or repeated themes. Chapter 4 would include what key answers you got from your interviewees and how they appeared within the text. These themes are your findings that generate your conclusions.

Starting from Chapter 3 would mean that you want to excel in a particular methodology. This will help you do an excellent job to understand a particular methodology, and understand all the consequences of selecting such methodology.

Sometimes you may want to do a survey on a particular topic, and you want to ask a few questions that can be part of a research study. This can be a great chance for you to conduct the survey you have always wanted to do, and at the same time, complete your thesis. Here, it becomes an opportunity to make the survey you wanted and a full journey that meets an academic requirement. It is a chance to fulfill a research need that you once had without proper guidelines.

Start with Interesting Findings – Ch. 4

A great thesis can start from where you want to find out about your topic. You start thinking about your topic from what data you want to reach. You start thinking about what outcomes you want to discuss in your study and then work backward to make your research question.

Remember reverse engineering, when you start from the end and then drive back to your original question. If you want to find the road from your home to your work, you can think about the return routes and they will tell you how to get there. Looking at the route from the end can give you insights into how you should take your journey.

For example, let us say you are interested in knowing people's opinions about your company's product. Consider what customers will say about your product and then start to see what questions can generate these answers. This route will give you the chance to rework your methodology to fit your exact informational needs.

The driving interest in this method is that you are focused on the final data that will be reached at the end of the study. You will make sure that you will be analyzing the exact data you want, and therefore have a roadmap for your thesis.

If you start with Chapter 4, you may have to move afterward to a different chapter. For example, you may want to get customer opinions about your product. Then you want to move to Chapter 3 to decide whether you want to use surveys, existing data, or in-depth interviews. After that, you will check the literature to choose a particular method that best serves your purpose. Another route can look at Chapter 2 after deciding on what you want to see in Chapter 4. This can facilitate Chapter 3.

Starting from Chapter 4 can work well if you have in mind what type of data you want to get. Then you have to do the reverse engineering to find possible routes to get to Chapter 1. It is just like a maze where you have to use trial and error. The great thing about it is that it works. It gives you what you want at the beginning instead of being surprised after collecting data and discovering you didn't get the desired findings.

Sometimes, if you do chapters 1, 2, and 3 in classic fashion, you may be surprised to see the findings. Sometimes, you want to think about the exact findings early to make sure you are in the path you want. Keeping your goal in mind from the beginning helps your planning and assures the desired findings. If you do not plan it correctly, and your proposal is approved based on Chapters 1, 2 and 3, and you did not get the data you want, you will then realize that you have wasted your time.

Whether you start from Chapter 4 or reach it sequentially, thinking about the collected data at an early stage is very important. Remember the *search for gold* story. Chapter 4 will point to the gold. You want to make sure that you get what you want after chapters 1, 2, and 3.

Chapters 1 will take you time to think and develop. Then Chapter 2 comes with its associated literature. Then Chapter 3 keeps you focused on the tools and methods to achieve your questions. You could find yourself in Chapter 3 with a set of questions that are not exactly related to your research question in Chapter 1. Furthermore, you may find out that your findings are not what you wanted at the beginning of the process.

Think about a recent trip to the supermarket. You initially had something in mind to buy. As you spend time in the supermarket, you end up with things you did not want. What's worse is to leave the supermarket without what you wanted initially. Having a movie and popcorn on your shopping list is better than going with the research question: what to buy at the supermarket.

In summary, it is helpful to think carefully about what you really want in Chapter 4 early in the process. Understanding which data is going to come after the research process can be as important as everything else. If you do not get the findings you want, then fixing it can be very expensive and time-consuming. You will have to do the research, questionnaire, interviews, or observations again.

Where Do You Want to End – Ch. 5

What is the theory with which you want to conclude? Sometimes it makes sense to have a personal statement or theory that your research study wants to prove and reach. This theory explains a phenomenon, a state, a relationship, a fact, or anything you have a particular opinion on.

For example, you may have a theory that says an employee's age affects customer satisfaction. Then this will be your conclusion that you believe to be true. It is your hypothesis that you want to test, and, therefore, your research question would be to discover the relationship between employee age and customer satisfaction. Your methodology would be a survey that measures employees' age, and customers' satisfaction with different companies. Then reach a conclusion whether customer satisfaction has any relationship with employee's age.

Here's another example. You have a theory that says commercial advertising makes the TV program less popular. You want to see how to tackle this theory as a research study. Your research question would be to ask what makes TV programs popular or unpopular. You would then look at the literature and start finding research about popular TV programs, and find that little is mentioned about advertising. You start your methodology by observing TV programs and measuring the amount of advertising per TV program. Then you measure the popularity of each of these TV programs. At this point, you could probably establish a relationship that concludes the opposite is true.

The more TV programs are popular, the more companies want to advertise during the program. This makes sense, but you may want to tackle it differently and reach a conclusion that it is not as popular as it could be.

It is important to think about your conclusions at an early stage of your research. You do not want to start your research without having an idea about what your research can end up suggesting. Possible conclusions coming from the research should be known from the beginning of your study.

A good conclusion is the one that you believe could be true. Those who oppose truth would be eager to read your study. Your research will provide them with evidence of your theory if it turns out to be true. Your conclusion would stress your theory on how the world we live in operates.

Your Proposal

Once you have decided on your topic, you need to have a proposal. The objective of the proposal is to get a green light to start your research. Many programs require you get approval for your proposal before starting your research. Those programs that do not require a proposal will require the research be approved by your advisor. It is important to receive appropriate approval proceeding with your research.

The proposal approval means that you are on the right track. Sometimes a small piece of advice can make a huge difference in your research. Therefore, never miss an opportunity to get advice on your proposal. Preparing a well-considered plan will make your research journey much easier.[7]

The proposal may also require that you get an institutional review board (IRB) approval. The IRB ensures that your research is legal and ethical. You may need to check with your program guidelines. Some regulations may prevent you from researching human subjects. The objective is to protect the welfare of the research subjects from any harm. Sometimes it may be psychologically difficult for kids if you research their sufferings. Overall, you need to make sure that your subjects will not suffer from your research.

The IRB may want to check that you have an informed consent form. This form is part of the survey or interview paperwork. The informed consent form is a document that the study participant has to read and sign before participating. It basically says that the participant understands the purpose of the study, the participation procedure, the estimated time, associated risks or benefits, the withdrawal procedure, and how to contact the researcher.

Part of the IRB check is to assure the privacy of participants. You may have to describe how participants' privacy and confidentiality is maintained and guaranteed. This may also need to be explained to the participant before participation. Evidence may be required to be presented to the IRB committee in order to get their approval.

IRB approval is required to be obtained before you start your data collection. If you are running a pilot study, you have to have a green light from the IRB before starting.

In addition, some programs may require you to have your proposal checked by an Academic Review Board (ARB) before you can start the study. The ARB will check your proposal, and may provide you with feedback. Then you can move on with your research.

Your proposal includes your chapters 1, 2 and 3. While these chapters may be developed further as you research the end of your journey, they should also include all the needed information to understand your entire research plan. The proposal needs to be in future tense, while the final submission of your thesis or dissertation will be in past tense since the research is finished.

Even if you are not required to spell your data collection instrument as part of your proposal, you need to include it. It is important that your proposal gives a clear idea of your plan so that once you get an OK, then you will not go back.

I call the data collection instrument your ticket to finish the research journey. Without this ticket, you are not ready for the next step. A good data collection instrument means a good plan to finish your journey exists. Until receiving this ticket, you will keep checking the available routes to finish your study.

Some programs may require you to attach your proposal several other documents. For example, you may have to include a plagiarism check report to make sure that no copy and paste was conducted without proper citations. You may have to include a training certificate on research ethics and acceptable behaviors. You may have to complete a self-assessment academic review checklist. The IRB approval may be required. They may also require a human subject's certificate. This can be an online exam to check that you understand how to protect participants' welfare. If you are conducting your research on private property, you may have to provide signed permission. If you are using someone else's survey or any copyrighted material, you may have to include permissions.

The proposal may also include a timeline of what you will do. You should follow this timeline to finish your thesis as soon as possible. Do not include a timeline that you know you will not follow. The more reasonable your timeline, the better the chance that you and your advisor will stick to it.

CHAPTER 2: THE JOURNEY

Your Advisor

While some programs would assign an advisor to you, other will give you the option to choose from a list of advisors. In the first case, you do not have an option other than to work with your assigned advisor and strive to find common interests. In the latter option, you will have a limited option to select from a range of advisors. The advantages of the latter option are limited and not so great. As you are yet to work with someone, you probably do not have much knowledge of how he or she would work with your particular needs and aspirations. [8]

In either case, you will have to make the relationship fruitful so that you earn your degree. The relationship should be a lasting mutual benefit relationship where you get your degree, and your advisor enjoys working with you. This will require you to manage the relationship and keep it effective and efficient.[9]

What does your advisor want? Your advisor wants to help you become a master or a doctor. This is a strong motivation for advisors. Not to mention any compensation, your advisor will earn for his or her time spent with you.

In addition, your advisor will be looking for possible co-authoring opportunities on future journal articles where you will be the author and your advisor will be a co-author. Depending on how much work you end up doing to publish the journal article, other people may be also involved in this publication.

Moreover, your advisor will enjoy the ideas that come with your truth-finding journey. The advisor may be able to make use of their time with you for their own research projects or other work they may be doing.

Sometimes, your research project will be part of other research that your advisor is working on. This is normal when the program receives grants to conduct research. Having a sponsor for your research may require the advisor to supervise your work that will be ultimately provided to another entity.

Some programs require advisors to have a minimum or a maximum number of students to supervise during their research. Therefore, the advisor is working with you to cross another item on their to-do list.

On the other hand, what do you want from your advisor? You want many things from your advisor. Mainly, you want to get your degree. The only way to get your degree is with your advisor's approval of your work.

You probably want time from your advisor. The more time you get, the more you can accomplish. However, the amount of time you need cannot be done in one shot, but rather a series of meeting as your thesis progresses.

While you want to get the advisor's OK on your project, this is normally time-consuming for your advisor because he or she will need to read your work, discuss it with you to get a better understanding, and provide you with advice on how your research can go further.

Therefore, you need to be very efficient managing the time your advisor will spare for you. The bargaining power lies with your advisor, so you need to adjust to his or her schedule. The worst that can happen is to have to fire your advisor, or them firing you.

Working with the advisor is like a covenant marriage; it should be once and for good. Finding another advisor can require a start over for your research topic. In addition, a new advisor could be concerned about working with you now that you have had a previous relationship with another advisor.

I once had to call several people to check on a student who wanted to work with me after a separation from another advisor. Recalling the experience, there was an issue that I needed to overcome to continue working with this individual. Advisors normally know what they are doing, while students do not realize that as much as they should.

As you work with your advisor, you will realize that much of the thesis or dissertation frustration is not associated with your advisor, but rather with the way you are tackling the research journey. After all, it is the student's research journey, not that of the advisor.

How do you establish a relationship with your advisor? There are contracts that some programs offer, or you can find one online that specifies the relationship details. These contracts will include general highlights identifying the expectations of each party. Here are some samples:

> The advisor commits to read "X" number of times the full proposal and give feedback within a "Y" number of days.

> The advisor will answer email questions within two business days.

> The advisor can meet "X" number of hours per week or month, up to a maximum of "Z" hours per six months.

You can see from these examples, the advisor's available time and effort are the focus.

On the other hand, the contract may include the student's responsibilities in progressing according to a timeframe. Such as:

> The student will only submit an edited work to the advisor.

> The student will be responsible for submitting drafts per the deadlines, and notify ahead of time if they cannot meet a deadline.

> Student commits to never disappear for "X" number of weeks without updating the advisor.

Again, these examples focus on the advisor's time.

Be respectful of your advisors' time and responsibilities outside the process. Do not expect work beyond written committed responsibilities even if your advisor goes above and beyond for a while. Your advisor's available time will probably change over the course of the thesis, and you cannot expect the same commitment throughout the journey.

What is another way to maintain a good relationship with your advisor? The answer is easy: do a great job! As your journey becomes interesting, your advisor will help you make it even better. If your journey turns out to be mismanaged, or unplanned, then your advisor will be the troublemaker from your perspective.

How do you plan for meeting with your advisor? Be well prepared. Your meeting should start like this, "I have finished doing "X", and I am planning to do "Y" and "Z." Your advisor will then have the chance to comment saying, "This is great, go ahead." Alternatively, the advisor may provide you with advice on what you should do differently. Do not expect your advisor to answer a question on what you are supposed to do next.

You have done something great for your advisor by reading this book. You are learning how to manage the journey. Therefore, just do what you have learned, and implement it. Then let your advisor see your plans and logic, and comment on them.

This is a great way to get your advisor's approval because the better organized you are in your presentation, the more your advisor will trust you to do the things you believe are best. If you do not know what you are doing, then you will face conflicts between what your advisor is telling you to do and how you should be proceeding.

If you know what you are doing, and you convey it to your advisor, he or she will comment on your plan from an advisor's perspective. The advisor will also make suggestions about the goal of your research.

If you do not know exactly what you want to do, then comments from the advisor will not convince you. This will lead to your advisor being disappointed in your performance because you basically did not do what you have been requested to do. What will happen is that you will be commenting on the advisor's previous comments.

Seek your advisor's direction in the methodology section. He or she can give you the best route to your findings. However, this may not be the only route. You may have your own plan. If so, then you have to articulate it well and show it to your advisor. Good plans will be approved unless major flaws exist. But if you plan it well, the comments you receive will be very valuable to you as a future researcher.

In short, you have to drive. Do not let your advisor drive. Your advisor can be seated in the back of the car, and offered the opportunity to agree or disagree in a timely manner. Do not turn left and then ask for approval. Ask for it ahead of the turn and you both will stay in agreement on how to proceed.

By the way, your advisor is not a navigation system in your journey. We do not have computer aided advising yet. Your advisor is also not your parent either. He or she will not take your call every time you get lost. Your advisor is similar to the examiner at the driver's license office.

How much valuable advice can one get from an advisor? In fact, much can be gained from the advisor. It depends on your hard work and focus. The advisor has normally worked with other students and has seen several research papers from start to finish. Therefore, he or she can help you with the smallest details that make your work excellent. You just need to give your advisor that chance. At the same time, advisors are looking for great work that you can provide. Therefore, they will help you at every level of your project.

On the other hand, if you are barely moving with your topic, do not expect them to do your work. In fact, they may decide to drop you to another advisor and spend the time on something else. The driver's license authority has the power to send you back to driving school, an option many advisors wish they had. In fact, some programs require students to go back to school if they do not show progress within a specified time.

If you travel to a new city and you hire a tour guide there, this tour guide can help you much. In fact, anyone in that place can provide you with valuable advice for a simple reason; they know its culture and they know its language. The same thing applies to your advisor. What matters is that you know where you want to go, and what you want to do there.

Nevertheless, there are differences among advisors that you may want to consider, such as their work experience, research experience, industry interest, topic knowledge, areas of expertise, availability, working style, personality traits, passion for research, methodology expertise, available resources, communication skills, the level of sophistication, etc..

It is a good suggestion to get advice about your advisor from your classmates and alumni. Look up advisors' previous mentees and talk to them. Take a class with the advisor if possible, or attend a workshop, or a seminar they are doing. Get to know their research interests by looking at their previous work. Ask them about their expectations and perceptions of your topic or thesis.

You need to know your advisor's strengths and weaknesses. Knowing your advisor's strengths and weaknesses will help you identify on what you should be focused.

For example, your advisor might be a statistician. This will mean you have to nail your thesis statistics well with their help and not be frustrated if he or she tells you to go back and fix errors. Your advisor may be an editor. In that case, never send your paper to your advisor unless you have first consulted with another editor, otherwise you will be spending time working on your grammar skills during your journey. But by the time you graduate, you will notice that your writing has dramatically improved, as you made sure your writing was great before submitting to your advisor for review.

On the other hand, if you know your advisor is weak at statistics, then you know you will need an expert statistician to help you with your statistics. You are probably going to have a statistician among your committee members, or your examiner will flag statistical issues in your final product. Such flags can be very costly. The worst that can happen is that you redo the methodology. Your analysis will also need to be updated, as well as your conclusions.

Your Committee

Your committee members are a third party that is involved in your journey for control reasons. The committee is there to make sure you did the work and you did not do something inappropriate. At the same time, it checks that the advisor has approved your work and it is at an acceptable level. The program wants this committee to be part of the quality control team to make sure that your final thesis or dissertation is acceptable by more than you and your advisor. Therefore, when it is published and it has the university stamp on it, it does not turn out to be a useless thesis.

Different programs may have different policies on how to handle this quality control component of your thesis. Some would have you choose your committee members, while other may choose them for you. Some programs use an "examiner" who is responsible for checking your work and provide feedback that has to be implemented before you pass. Some examiners have the power to base part of your entire grade on your thesis. Some have internal examiners and external examiners. Some programs have a blind internal examining team that will assign your thesis to someone you don't know, and this person will receive your thesis without your name or other identifiable references. An external examiner is someone from outside the university who acts as an independent reviewer as part of the quality assurance strategy.

Your best friend is your advisor. The committee's comments go to your advisor who may not have pinpointed the same comment to you, or failed to instruct you to correct it. Your advisor will likely agree with every comment made by the committee and require you to make corrections.

In rare occasions, your advisor may be in disagreement with the committee due to different schools of thought, different perceptions of what is more accurate or other opinion differences. Even in these cases, following your advisor's comments should help you get your degree. In addition, your advisor will probably spend much more time with your study than any other committee member.

A committee member can help you a lot. The best help they can provide is in areas in which your advisor is weak. If your advisor is weak at statistics, then your committee member can help you in that area. Your committee member can act as a backup in case your advisor disappears. In addition, a committee member can help your advisor overcome possible differences in opinion. I remember my advisor was very comfortable with my final dissertation after he read the positive feedback I got from another committee member. The committee member provided additional support for my advisor to accept my dissertation. Sometimes your advisor will act like a perfectionist until such moments.

The Writing Process

The obvious advice is to write, write, and write. The research process will keep you on a learning journey, and this journey is not only reading and learning, rather it is doing, analyzing, and finding. Therefore, you need to understand that the writing process includes writing what you are doing, and what you are analyzing.

Keep It Simple and Short

The best way to get going with your thesis is to find a working template and follow it. Many programs provide the template as part of the thesis description and requirement guide. The template defines the headlines of your thesis. To complete the template, you will have to write a minimum or a maximum number of words or pages depending on your program. That is the last thing you want to worry about now.

What is important at the beginning is to write your main ideas down in the template. Just write a sentence or two under each headline. This is your start, to fill in the main milestones. At the least, you need to know your final destination and the main headlines to your destination. Do not worry now about a specific reference or a great statement. What is important is to pour your main ideas on paper.

As you build your thesis, remember to write what is needed. Never use "fill in" words to make it look long. Keep the important information as you focus on finishing the thesis. In addition, the more details it contains, the more costly it becomes to edit, correct and review. Your advisor will probably prefer it to be short, at least in the early stages.

As you get closer to the end of the journey, feel free to elaborate on the different components, as necessary. At a later stage, you will have all of your content in your head, and need to write it down. But at the beginning, you do not know the full picture. Moreover, your advisor will probably be giving you more directions in the early stages, as you develop your plan.

Time Management

You want to finish your thesis, and get your degree. Deadlines work. You need to create a timetable and stick to it. You need to share your timetable with those around you. As others realize that you have a deadline, they can help you achieve your objective. You can also read more about time management, and follow the tips provided by self-development techniques and how to follow a schedule.

Part of your time management is to get your advisor to push you to finish your thesis. Your advisor will follow your time management. If you set deadlines for yourself and share them with your advisor, you will stick to them to meet your advisor's expectations. This can help you work on your thesis, at the same time; you will be getting feedback from your advisor on your progress.

There are several tools available to help boost your productivity. For example, find an editor that can help you proofread your material. Some students find a variety of software that works for them. Software you might use includes thesis generation software, a thesis template application, text to speech and speech to text types of software applications can also be helpful.

Depending on your needs, it is a good idea to hire people to assist you. You may want to hire research assistants, a secretary, survey participants, typewriters, editors, statisticians, analysts, and even advisors.

You may have a thesis or dissertation mentor who can help you just like the advisor if you feel that your advisor is not providing you the help you need. Sometimes, it is difficult or impossible to replace your advisor. You may want to hire a friend, a colleague, or alumni to assist you with your thesis. Someone who cares about you can give you direction and motivation to finish your thesis.

Each chapter has a different timetable. Pay attention to the time as you proceed with each chapter. For example, the time-consuming part of Chapter 1 is the final research questions. Once you start to have many research questions, you know you are wasting your time. Just keep the number of research questions small and proceed. You can come back later.

Chapter 2 can be a never-ending journey reading all types of literature. You want to have a story to tell about the literature. Then you write it in your Chapter 2. Sometimes you will find a list of research articles that you want to include in your literature review and there is an urge not to exclude any of them. This is a trap. You need to limit the literature to what most important for the research.

Chapter 3 tends to be short. After you have the idea in your mind, you just spell it out with all the details you have in mind.

Chapter 4 can be a very long chapter if you want to get a Nobel Prize. Nevertheless, it should be a specific task to report your findings. This chapter can sound very boring. That is OK. This is neither fiction nor non-fiction book. It is a thesis that shows you know how to research. In this chapter, just write down what you found. Describe the results, and provide analysis of these findings.

For every finding in Chapter 4, you will interpret what it means in Chapter 5. Every recommendation you have should come from Chapter 4. As you follow Chapter 4, you know you will finish

Chapter 5 on time. Every time you do not follow Chapter 4 headings, you will lose a lot of time.

It is important that you finish as soon as possible. Leave a space for your advisor to comment. Your advisor's comments can limit the remaining time to finish your thesis. Even if you feel that some time is missing, proceed.

If you feel you do not know what more to do, it means you have finished. You need to send your work to your advisor, and your advisor will tell you what you need to do next. Do not leave the ball in your court. Throw it to your advisor saying, "I have finished this part." Let your advisor tell you want you need to do instead of you trying to guess what remains.

Remember, this is a journey. It does not have to be a trip to the moon. It can be a short journey to a nearby park. What is important is that you take it. It does not have to be long, even if your program requires you to have a minimum number of pages or words. The length of your thesis should be your last concern. You can think about it during the research process, but it should not be an issue until you finish your research. What really matters is that you get your idea right and your advisor is OK with it.

Procrastination is a disease that you need to overcome. If you take a trip, you want to take a full advantage of your time during the trip. If you procrastinate, the joy of your trip will be lost. If you slow down your journey, your advisor may forget much of your work. When you travel, you want to reach your destination as soon as possible, and minimize transit time. Procrastination is similar to the time wasted when a flight is canceled. No one wants a flight canceled on a journey.

Will you need to take time off work to finish? Perhaps, and this is a valid option if you feel that you literally do not have sufficient time. It is better to take it sooner rather than later after having fallen behind. How do you know if you have fallen behind? Check with your classmates. You always want to be competitive with your classmates. Stay in touch with them, and stay updated with their progress. It can be great motivation for you to speed up to finish Chapter 1 if you see your friends have finished it. In addition, they will be happy to share their success with you in finishing Chapter 1 and may provide you with assistance.

Writing Style

Are you going to use APA style? If you do not know APA style[10] or any other style then you may want to check with your advisor if a writing style is suggested or required by your program.

APA is a writing style that dictates how your manuscript should look. It includes the formatting of your paper. For example, the writing style may indicate that you have to put the page number on the upper left-hand side of every page. The APA (American Psychology Association), made this style in order to standardize all papers. It helps authors to follow one set of rules to keep expectations on the same level.

A writing style also sets the standard for formatting headings, margins, font types and sizes, and many other details. Everything set in the writing style is to help the publication be more effective. For example, graphs, charts, and figures can be confusing on a black and white photocopy. Therefore, the writing style has a suggestion on how to make it clear.

In short, following a writing style helps your thesis or dissertation move to a standard level manuscript. It also gives valuable advice on how your writing should look and sound. It will address writing issues that you may not have thought of, such as citations, references, paraphrasing, and quotations. For example, it describes the best way to address a YouTube reference.

The writing style will provide you with general principles in academic writing. It will describe how to avoid bias and to use common practices. It describes how and when to address first, second, and third parties in your manuscript. It also describes how to deal with mathematical formulas. Moreover, it lists general principles of writing ethics and how to make sure you do not commit an act of academic dishonesty.

Editors

The easiest criticism of your paper is a spelling mistake or a grammatical error. It provides easy, superficial indicators of the quality of your entire work. A reader will easily catch these small mistakes and generalize that your research is poor.

Editors know their job better than you do, even if you believe you are a good writer. Editors who edit theses and dissertations have experience with academic requirements. For example, you may confuse the use of a word in a specific setting. You may not be aware of a writing style requirement in a table or chart. You may need help in formatting a Table of Contents. There are many issues that editors have come across that you have not. The time lost between the dates when your paper is submitted, and being returned to you for writing issues can cost you time and money.

Finding an editor can be as easy as asking your advisor, or a classmate. Alumni from the same program would be a great source of advice. Many programs have editors who have worked with previous students. They may have been hired several times to the point they become familiar with the program requirements. These people can also provide you with hints into issues you need to correct because they have worked with students both before and after they get comments from the program. They become experts in what is required. You can also seek freelancers online. They can be very effective and for reasonable fees.

Editors may charge per project, per page or per word count. Depending on an editor's level of professional training, experience, and education, their rates vary.

Related Community

When you earn your thesis or dissertation, you will also earn a degree. This degree means that you have accumulated knowledge in a specific field of study. This specialization and earned degree should open new doors for you.

What will you do after you get your degree? You continue to do what you have been doing. You may keep the same job, for the same company, doing the same thing. Well, this is a possible answer, but for you, it may not be the desired answer. The desired answer is that you will change the world with your education and you will eventually get the Nobel Prize as discussed earlier.

Now, you can think realistically about the next step. Let us say you will become an expert in your subject matter. For you to be an expert, you need to appear in locations where other experts appear. So now is the best time to start appearing in these locations.

Reach out to your study topic community. For example, you may find organizations that could provide you with membership. This membership can be very timely during your thesis or dissertation journey because, they will be offering the help you need. You may join their social network and get in touch with others who have similar interests in your topic.

When you get in touch with the community, you open up more opportunities for yourself, not just for the thesis. You may attend a conference, a gathering, a discussion session, etc. These will give you the motivation to pursue your research. It will also give you insights into your research topic. You will also gain access to the network that can open opportunities.

It is a great opportunity for you to talk about your research topic. It will help build your confidence and your communication skills. You can even present your findings. This will give you the proper experience and authority in your research topic.

This community does not have to be an academic one. While academic conferences are great, you can also attend non-academic activities. For example, you may find a local NGO that is interested in your topic. You may reach out to clubs, chambers, specialized institutions, social clubs or any other type of gathering that is interested in your topic, directly or indirectly.

Conferences

Search for a conference that you can attend and make a presentation about your topic. Attending and presenting at a conference is a goal you need to think about and plan when it would be suitable to do; now, later, or after you finish your program. Starting this search early can help you in several aspects.

Firstly, if you attend a conference on your subject matter, you will probably see many people at your stage in life that are seeking degrees, preparing research, or searching for the truth about a certain topic. This can be a great opportunity to discuss with these people your research interests, and they may provide you with great advice and support.

Secondly, if you attend a conference, you will get the spirit of your degree. It is a feeling that tells you that you can do it. It has to do with the intrinsic motivation of reaching your goals.

Societies and Organizations

Search for societies and organizations that are related to your research topic. Joining such organizations can provide you with access to experts on your topic. It is helpful to check the calls for papers, current research, featured topics, awarded individuals, news and updates. These will help you stay in touch with the community. Doing so can provide important insight towards your research. Some memberships to these organizations may also provide you with access to publications, conferences, events, and access to the network.

Prizes and Awards

While you are preparing your thesis, search for awards or prizes related to your topic. You may indeed win one but will never know unless you try. Perhaps more importantly, searching for awards and prizes can open the door for you to learn what research is in demand. Some of the organizations offering awards are fulfilling their organizational goals by doing so.

Life Journey

Family & Kids

The research project can be very time-consuming. At times, it may be an emotional challenge and some thesis candidates face depression when loved ones suffer because of the journey. Some tips that can help deal with the demands of a research journey include the following: time management, taking time off work, spending quality time with your family and kids, and taking time off your research project. Finding balance is a key.

You need family support. Everyone needs to understand that writing a thesis is a time-consuming journey that offers a great return for the entire family. Your family needs to know that they are part of your success in the journey. Celebrate the milestones of your project with your family. Set aside family time on periodical bases so they know when it is their time. Take time for your family during the weekend and go out. Establish a routine schedule so everyone knows when it is family time. If you choose to work on your project a few hours a day, keep the same hours every day so they get used to you being away during this time.

Work

Your work can be a source of success, and your research study may help your career advance. Many choose their career as their source of inspiration, and the practical beneficiary of their research study. Therefore, you need to make the best of it. However, do not let your work turn your research project into a nightmare. When you do your project, keep it independent from your work. Do not link your work with your research project. Remember, this is an educational journey that expects you to learn, not to reach conclusions.

Your work may provide you with access to participants and resources to conduct your study. It may sponsor your research and pay for budgets needed to complete your study. Your work may also provide you with access to industry experts that can influence the findings of the study.

You need to balance the integrity of your study with your work objectives when competing agendas float to the surface. Your work requirements can influence the writing you do. You may be tempted to use your research paper as evidence to prove a point in your workplace. This conflict can damage the integrity of your study.

Any challenge to the integrity of your study means that you did not learn how to do proper research. In addition, this conflict between work and study means conflict between your education and your career. These should complement each other, not contradict each other.

University

Your university can provide you with many services. Make sure to take advantage of all of that is offered. The university can provide access to up-to-date research, access to instructors and experts, access to student services such as editors, proofreaders, online resources, tutorials and others.

A university librarian can be very resourceful in getting books you need. They know methods to get books that you don't. Check online resources. Some online databases are accessible only from your campus computer network. Your program may provide you with a username and password to access these online libraries.

Sponsors

Finding a sponsor for your research is a valuable exercise. You need to set expectations in advance so that your sponsor understands that writing a thesis is an educational journey and that your thesis objective is to earn a degree, but that your findings may help your sponsor. You need to make sure your advisor is involved in finding and choosing a sponsor. Once again, advisor support is an essential part of your thesis project. The type of reporting required by your sponsor may be a lot different from the program-required reporting, and your advisor should be aware of the differences.

The experiences gained when having a sponsor are many. You become an expert in your field, you build your network, and you have the opportunity to take this journey with you to the next level. You also have a significant study since a sponsor is highly interested in your research findings.

However, do not let a sponsor interfere in your research project to the point where your study is no longer a fact-finding research project, causing your advisor to lose interest in working with you. Rather, the research project needs to be a win-win-win situation where you, your advisor, and your sponsor all benefit from the research project journey.

CHAPTER 3: THE THEORY

Theory and Practice

So what does "theory" mean? Have you heard of *Theory* X or *Theory* Y? These were developed by Douglas McGregor to explain people's motivation at work. Here is *Theory* X.

Theory X asserts that some managers if you could read their minds, you would find an idea that says that employees are inherently lazy, are stupid, dislike work, find every chance to slack off, prefer taking breaks, find excuses, and avoid responsibility. Does your manager agree with this idea? Do your parents? What about your teachers? Is this theory even true?

Let's consider *Theory* Y. *Theory* Y asserts that some managers believe employees are creative by nature. They love work, and they usually try their best to achieve higher results. Employees are hard-working, ambitious, motivated, and willing to go the extra mile to make sure they are doing their best. *Theory* Y managers believe that employees only need direction, guidance, and support to achieve higher results. This idea exists only subconsciously and drives their behavior. Do you have a manager who believes in *Theory* Y? Perhaps someone at work, a parent, a teacher, or a coach?

These two theories provide different perspectives on how the world operates. They provide an understanding about management and how to effectively motivate people. *Theory* X managers usually believe that control is very important, and support using mandatory employee attendance systems, and that detailed, specific directions are necessary for employee productivity.

On the other hand, *Theory Y* managers are likely to support organizations providing employees with the tools and guidelines to elevate their productivity, and that employees need advisors who assure tools are available for people to work effectively.

It is important for people to understand these two theories. They help us understand how organizations operate, and they assist us in addressing work issues. Managers who have learned about these theories sometimes rethink their assumptions about employee behavior. They attempt to explain managerial behavior as well as organizational dynamics and provide data to support their assertions[11]

But are these theories or facts? A researcher needs to provide evidence to support his or her theory and may need to conduct a research study to produce the needed evidence. You may even be able to provide evidence from your own life that supports *Theory X* or *Theory Y*.

In the previous example, these theories come from social sciences. Social sciences deal with people and their behaviors. What about chemistry or physics? These subjects would have a completely different set of rules and examples.[12]

For example, in physics, your theory may say that movement generates electric current. Then you go test it in the lab and provide evidence. Scientific research methods say that you need to have a hypothesis, and then use lab testing results to accept or reject the hypothesis.

Here's another example: assume you have a theory that says if you open the water tap, water will run out. Well, this is so obvious to the point we call it a law. It is similar to Newton's first law that says objects remain in their state of motion.

Medical sciences require you to go to the lab to conduct your research. You may have to measure blood pressure or the presence of bacteria. The theory would say that a specific medication eliminates a certain bacteria. You then collect data from several patients and analyze it to see whether your hypothesis is accepted or rejected .

Your study may require a conceptual framework. This is the graphical diagram that shows your study. If you have independent and dependent variables, you need to put them on a diagram that shows their relationships. These can be very informative and help others to understand your theory. Your conceptual framework may be based on a theoretical framework that comes from the literature. A theoretical framework can be based on theory, law, principle, generalization or research findings. After you finish your study, the conceptual framework you developed may become someone else's theoretical framework.

It is important to include your concerns when writing your theory. You need to specify the nature of your research study, its scope or focus, its coverage area, timeframe, assumptions, limitations, delimitations, and any other information you believe is important for the reader to know about your truth-finding journey.

Inductive vs. Deductive

Inductive research is when you start from observations or collected data, then find a pattern that can generate a theory. Therefore, you explore data to find information to reach knowledge. The induction is when you realize phenomena from patterns of data. Qualitative approaches are generally inductive.

Deductive research is when you do the opposite. You start from theory, explain patterns or hypotheses, then observe the data that confirm it. Quantitative approaches are generally deductive.[13]

Mixed studies normally use both inductive and deductive approaches. They find data to construct a theory, and they confirm a theory by other data.

One theory says "..every action has a reaction." The deductive research approach might observe whether a thrown ball returns to the one who threw it. The inductive research approach might observe "Kid 1" hitting "Kid 2" then finding a pattern that confirms every time "Kid 1" hits "Kid 2", "Kid 2" hits back. Such patterns generate the theory that for every action, there is a reaction.

Contributing to Knowledge vs. Synthesizing

There are different notions in research. One says that a dissertation in a doctoral program should contribute to knowledge. In other words, you have to come up with something new. You have to confirm a new theory, or find a new phenomenon. You have your own theory of how the universe operates.

On the other hand, some believe that a master's thesis does not contribute to knowledge. Rather, it should synthesize information to produce a comprehensive overview of current knowledge.

The first notion seeks new theory, while the second only covers a topic well. A master's degree may accept a synthesis, while a doctoral program may require a contribution to knowledge. However, this may differ from one program to another. Also be aware that the British education system uses the term *thesis* to refer to doctoral work and *dissertation* for master's degree work. The opposite is true in the American system.

Logic and Fallacies

A very important objective of the thesis journey is to make sure that students draw conclusions based on logical reasoning. Logical reasoning means that everything you include in your thesis follows a clear logic from start to end. Your research question should be logical given the study problem.

In high school we learned if A is greater than B, then B is less than A. These types of logical arguments make up your conclusions and your methodology. For example, if rain occurs, then you order a pizza, it is not logical to assume ordering pizza is the cause of rain.

There are many logical flaws or defective arguments called fallacies. It is good for you to learn some common fallacies, just to stay away from them.

A thesis that allows a logical fallacy is of critically poor quality. Therefore, it is important to check the logic of your thesis. Sound logic is essential for a successful thesis or dissertation.

For example, a research question should be logically driven from the problem statement. A hypothesis should logically provide an answer to the research question. The research methodology should logically answer the research questions. The data collection tool should logically provide data that is valid to measure the study variables. A statistical finding should logically support the thesis implications or conclusions.

For example, if a research project is studying the relationship between employee pay and corporate profit, the researcher is trying to determine if companies that are more profitable pay higher salaries. Assume a research team prepares 1000 copies of an employee survey that are distributed to a large corporation's employees. The survey asks employees, "Do you believe that companies that are more profitable should pay higher salaries to their employees?"

I am confident you can predict the results of this study. The study results likely confirm a significant relationship between employee pay and company profits. However, survey questions can never be used to reach such a conclusion.

The logical flaws in this example are clear if you think about it. At the same time, this research question can be approached many different ways. While you could use a survey, it may make more sense to just use secondary data. Running a correlation between company profit and average salary from the annual report is more logical.

Bias

Be careful not to fall into conflicts of interest. Once you find yourself having to discuss the researcher, then you know you are falling into a conflict of interest that does not help your study. Once you, as a person, have something to do with the research process, then you know there is a conflict of your personal interest with the research interest. This opens the door for more conflict.

For example, assume you're researching your company, and you have scheduled an interview with your boss. This will eventually cause issues that either you or your boss finds uncomfortable. It is better to stay away from such scenarios. If your study requires an interview with your boss, get someone else to assist you with this procedure. Why? It may be difficult for you to analyze the interview objectively, and when it comes to writing the findings, the possibility of justifying yourself, and reporting the boss inaccurately could threaten the credibility of your thesis.

People have a tendency to use research papers in an attempt to prove their personal theories about work. For example, assume you believe that your company is not providing enough training to employees. This viewpoint will naturally become part of your conclusion if you believe that upper management is not allowing lower management to participate in decision-making processes. You will find yourself addressing the importance of management by participation.

In Chapter 5, you have to stick to the findings in Chapter 4. Once you start to address topics outside of Chapter 4, then you probably have a self-interest in introducing these new topics. These topics do not help your study; rather think seriously about your honesty in interpreting the findings.

Good Science and Bad Science

The threat of *pseudoscience* is a major concern for researchers. Good science helps the world, while bad science confuses the world. You need to be careful not to fall into the trap of using pseudoscience in your thesis. Bad science will not only put your academic work at risk, but will also affect your reputation and people that surround you. Just like any other discipline, fraud is a concern.

Pseudoscience occurs when you try to hide the truth, make inaccurate claims, mislead your readers, manipulate findings, fabricate data, ignore important issues, or exaggerate the truth about your research.

Literature Review

The literature review indicates that you have researched your topic. It shows the list of research that has been done on your topic and how it tries to answer your research questions. A full literature review does not mean that you have read all the literature, but it says you read all the relevant information.

Relevant information is that which the reader of your research needs to know in relation to your research study. Almost every word of your research questions is addressed in your  literature review. For example, if your research is measuring employee satisfaction in low paying banking jobs in a geographical location, then your literature review needs to discuss employee satisfaction and dissatisfaction, job satisfaction differences between low paying and high paying banking jobs, banking industry employment dynamics, the nature of banking in your geographical location, employment engagements, labor laws and regulations, market conditions, consumer preferences, etc.

Your literature review needs to include existing theories or models relating to your study. For example, it should include motivation theories that describe employee satisfaction. It may also describe the characteristics of low paying vs. high paying jobs as well as human resource practices in low paying vs. high paying jobs. Other literature you may want to consider includes banker's code of conduct documentation, and research on both employee psychology in office jobs such as banking, and the nature of relationships between employee, company, and customer.

The literature review may also address research methods associated with your topic. For example, you need to cite all similar studies that used the same methodology you are using. If you are using a different methodology, you need to address literature that uses a similar methodology to yours.

In your literature review, you are not just listing what others are saying. Rather, you are indicating what others are saying about your research topic. Therefore, you will be bringing their inputs to your study. The literature review does not have to be all those who support your idea, it may also include the critics in your field of study. The objective is to provide a review of all the literature discussing your research questions.[14]

Searching Online

You are fortunate to do your research study in the age of Google, and Google Scholar. Please note: Google Scholar is nothing like Google Search. While Google Scholar has the power of Google Search in finding the information you seek, Google Scholar shows scholarly work only. This fact is very important because you need to gather academic research, not a blogger's personal opinions. Google Scholar allows you to download a reference in your desired format, provide insight about how many other research papers have cited this reference, and enable you to quickly skim the abstract.

The technology has completely transformed the research journey. Imagine in the past, people had to spend nights in a physical library, reading full books to find the relevant information. People needed to take courses on how to use the library, and how to search for relevant articles.

Now your research project is as simple as a click. Take a tutorial on how to search online. It is intuitive to search online, but going through a tutorial on searching can give you hints on how to find resources even faster. Also check out your university library's electronic database. Librarians can help you in the process if needed.

Relevant Studies

The key in your literature review is that you find relevant information that can help your literature review provide a complete picture of what others have said about your topic. This means that you will need to read many articles and choose those that are most effective and relevant. Abstracts provide great insights about articles that make research easier. Abstracts are available online even if you do not have access to the full articles and provide sufficient information about the content of an article.

Recent Literature

Check for recent literature. Some of the recent literature may not be as available as older literature. Nevertheless, you need to look for articles published within the last few years. Check your program requirements; a certain percentage of your reference list may have to be published within a specific year range. If you are doing your research now, you may as well check the latest literature about your topic.

Base Studies

Your study needs to have at least one base study, preferably recent. This base study can be your model as discussed previously. If you are replicating a study, then you already have decided on your base study. You will need to understand the base study just as you understand your own study. Your base study will provide you with the roadmap to your own study, making your research process clear and focused.

If you are not replicating a study, then you probably have a similar study in one or more components of your research. For example, you may be following a research methodology that is similar to another study. If that is the case, then that study is the base study for your methodology. Some may have a base study for the nature of research, the framework, the analysis, the hypothesis, etc.

Your base study needs to be recent. If you find a great base article that is old, then look up recent papers that cite it. You will probably find a recent paper that can be your base study.

In every field of study, there is classic literature that almost every study cites. These studies need to be in your literature review. You need to be familiar with foundation articles in your field of study.

The base study is your passport to finishing your research project successfully. A great base study will get you going smoothly. If you don't have a base study passport, then expect people to stop you and ask what are you doing and why it is important.

Base Authors

Not only do you need to have foundation articles, but you also need to be familiar with their authors. There are popular authors in every field of study. You need to know these authors, look up their websites and recent publications. Follow them on twitter. This process can provide a roadmap about the literature from their point of view. You may see their research questions over time to give you a direction of where researchers are going with their research.

You may be able to connect with these authors, and follow their steps. Read about their activities, their current research, and their upcoming events. These authors may work for research centers or work on editorial boards of journals. These could be a source of information that will help your literature review.

Reputable Journals

Your literature review needs to be based on reputable journals. Therefore, make sure that you find these journals, and read their calls for papers; maybe your paper will be among those called. This can be a great opportunity for you as you move on to the next level.

You want to make sure that your base article is published by a reputable journal. References coming from a non-reputable journal compromises the value and integrity of your thesis.

Have you heard of the impact factor? Journals have an impact factor. This impact factor is a metric used to measure how a specific journal is affecting a field of study. It is measured by how many articles cite this journal. The more articles that cite a specific journal, the higher the impact factor of that journal. Therefore, the journal's editorial board has an incentive to publish only those articles that are critical of the subject in order to maintain a high impact factor.

The Godfather

As you finish the research journey in your field of study, you should have a role model researcher that affected your research study. This is your Godfather. This person should be an author from whom you have learned much, have been influenced by his or her research, and someone whose work is highly related to your findings. If you do not have a Godfather, then you missed much about your journey. It is as if you traveled on vacation without having used an effective tour guide.

Your References

As you start your research journey, you will start to read and based on your reading, you will think, and based on your thoughts your final manuscript will be crafted. It is important to keep a list of all of your references by the time you finish your research.

Your list of references is important for several reasons. First, you have to have a list of references at the end of your research paper as per most programs' guidelines. Second, this list of references provides easy access to the journal articles or books that you cited in your paper. This is to help future researchers go back to original work that you believe is important to completely understand your claims. Third, this list provides the basis for your paper's claims. For example, if you believe that Einstein's theory of relativity is a founding research to your study, then you need to have it on your list. This way you give Einstein proper credit in your study. Fourth, as you list a work by Einstein in your paper, people looking for research that is building on Einstein's work will be able to find your research. Fifth, missing an important piece of literature from being cited in your references means that you did not fully cover that literature, at least to a certain extent.

Before you submit your final thesis or dissertation, you have to check that every citation you have in your paper is referenced. At the same time, every reference in your reference list should be also cited somewhere in your paper. Search for "references management software." The desktop version of Mendeley by Elsevier is great. It integrates well with MS Word. MS Word has its own reference management tool. If you are not using software, building and managing references can be very time-consuming, and will require you to manage your paper for references during the entire journey.

In all cases, you will need to have a list of references as you write. Every time you cite, you need to add the reference as you go. This will become a habit, and you may have a longer reference list than you actually need. Removing some references is much easier than finding a missing reference.

Have you heard of DOI? DOI is Digital Object Identifier. This is a code for most journal articles, which is a number for that specific manuscript. If you search a DOI, it will immediately provide you with a specific journal article. It is also required by some writing styles, such as APA writing style. It makes referencing much easier because searching for a DOI will provide access to its related reference immediately.

Note that not all journal articles have the same weight in the literature. Some journal articles are very popular because of their academic contribution to the field of study. Some journals are well known for their high-quality research. Having more of these references in your reference list will provide evidence of higher quality to your research paper. It indicates that you have built your research study based on research that is more reliable. This is not to discriminate against any non-reputable research journals, which also may have merit.

In addition, note that the reference list includes all cited works in your research, but your problem statement and your framework citations may be much more important than other citations in your general overview of the literature. Therefore, if you are concerned about selecting the best journals in your reference list, you may want to focus on the key citations in your research rather than the reference list itself.

Methodology

Your methodology is what you will do to answer your research questions, and accept or reject your hypothesis. It is the action in your journey. It may be your survey, your interviews, your experiment, or your research process. It is a plan for your information gathering process.

Your methodology can be a source of indecisiveness. Make a final decision about your methodology and once you decide how you will conduct your study, stick to it. What you do not want to do is change your methodology. Do not proceed with your research project until you have determined your methodology so that you do not have to go back and fix your entire research study, which will be necessary if you change your methodology.

Primary Data vs. Secondary Data

Primary data is the data you collect. For example, if you use a tape measure and record the length and width of your notebook, this is primary data. Secondary data is collected by someone else.

Secondary data includes census data by a government. Annual reports are secondary data reported by companies. Journal articles, reports, websites, and online databases are all examples of secondary sources of data.

When you run a survey or collect data that is a primary source of data. When you interview people and ask them questions, that is primary data. If you observe data by yourself, this another example of primary data. Conducting an experiment is also considered primary data.

Primary data is powerful because it can be customized to your exact research needs. For example, if you want to research whether a specific medication cures an illness, then you need to go and collect the data yourself. Pharmaceutical companies regularly conduct primary research. It would be difficult to use secondary data to measure such relationship.

Depending on your study, you may be able to reach your objective with secondary data. Sometimes you cannot do it without secondary data. Other times, you have to do your primary data.

Causation vs. Correlation

When it rains, you get wet. When it does not rain, you do not get wet. Every time it rains, you get wet. Of course, this occurs while you are outside, under the skies. This is causation. You can see the simple logic of every time X happens, then Y happens. If X does not happen, we never experience Y.

Correlation, on the other hand, is the fact that Y and X get together. It does not necessarily mean one affects the other. Rather, a third factor, such as Z influences them both. For example, you might get wet, and you might see a rainbow. These two correlate but they do not cause each other. The rain could cause both to happen, yet rain falls without producing a rainbow, and you can still get wet by means other than rainfall.

It is important to distinguish between a causal relationship and a correlative relationship. You have to be very specific when you use this terminology because its meaning is very different.

For example, as people get jobs their happiness is raised. Research may reach this conclusion after surveying people about their work status, and their happiness level. A relationship can be measured using correlation analysis and the correlation analysis may show a significant association between these two variables.

Yet, we cannot claim that because people have jobs, they are happy. Even though, it makes sense that when people have a job, their happiness increases. The causation conclusion requires much more work to prove, yet correlation can be sufficient to confirm your point, which says there is an association between having a job and one's happiness.

Qualitative vs. Quantitative

Qualitative research occurs when you explore. The key idea is to explore or find out. On the other hand, quantitative research occurs when you want to examine. The key idea is *examination.*

Qualitative research will give you the opportunity to go deep into a subject and investigate what is call phenomena. A phenomenon is a fact that appears to you upon your research. If you open your eyes after the rain, you may see a rainbow. This phenomenon appears in the sky. You may need to explore this phenomenon and write your thesis about it. So all the people who come after you can build on the phenomena you found.[15]

Quantitative research will give you the opportunity to collect data about something specific to reach a generalization. For example, if you had discovered the rainbow, you may decide to collect data about it. You may then have concluded that there is an association between rain and rainbows. The generalization, a rainbow always appears after the rain, would have been new knowledge that the study found.

In qualitative research, you may use an interview, observations, and deep digging on a fact-finding journey. While in quantitative research you may survey, measure, and check a specific phenomenon to reach a lasting conclusion.

Mixed Method

A mixed study occurs when you want to achieve both quantitative and qualitative research simultaneously. For example, you want to investigate the colors that appear in the sky after rain. You may want to explore the topic first. Then you reveal the rainbow. After that, you want to generalize this phenomenon by conducting quantitative research.

Here's another example: you may be wondering why students do poorly on their exams. You may want to explore this phenomenon by interviewing students who do poorly in their exams. During this journey, you find out they have many absences. Now you can say that you found a pattern that students who have done poorly on their exams missed many classes. Then you want to generalize that students who attend classes do better on their exams. This generalization requires a quantitative research to examine and to verify that student performance is related to student attendance. Then you can survey students in a variety of circumstances, places and situations. The survey will check their performance and their attendance. After that, statistical tests will be conducted to reach a conclusion that this relationship was not due to coincidence.

Variable Operationalization

Let's say your hypothesis asserts that people who suffer obesity tend to be more aggressive. Now, you have two variables: obesity and aggression. How do you measure these two variables? Obesity can be measured by a person's body fat percentage. What about aggression? The concept of aggression is not easy to measure so you have to find a way to operationalize this variable. If you examine the literature, you may find an aggression scale. The aggression scale may be 5 survey questions that ask about a person's willingness to fight, tease, or confront others. These questions would specifically measure your variable and make it operational.

You will need to check the literature and see how other researchers have measured your variable. You may find several scales that fit your research. You may have to create your own scale to operationalize a variable. If you make it yourself, you may want to check its validity and reliability by running a pilot study.

Pilot Study

Why do you do a pilot study? You do it in order to make sure that your methodology will generate the desired results. It is reliability and validity check for your research method. You do not want to conduct your research method on your entire sample, and then achieve results contrary to what you wanted.

For example, you have developed a survey that no one else has tested before to achieve a specific objective. You are planning to run the survey over hundreds of participants. You may want to run this survey on a small number of participants in a pilot study.

In the pilot study, you basically conduct a qualitative mini research. You will be giving your survey to a few individuals who will answer the survey. Then you may sit with these participants, and make sure that they understood the survey questions correctly. Then, you will make sure that the way they answer the survey questions is exactly how the questions are intended to be answered.

During the pilot study, there is a good chance that you will better understand your topic. You may realize that you need to remove, modify, or add a question. You may want to re-word the questions so that it implies the intended purpose of the question. Alternatively, you may realize you want to go one step backward to achieve your purpose.

A pilot study is needed every time you do not have enough evidence that your questions have been tested. If you have translated questions from another language, then you need to test the translation. If you have modified an existing survey, you want to make sure it holds the same level of validity. If you have developed your own questions, you want to make sure they are valid and can achieve their desired results.

During the pilot study, you will get a mini result of your research. These mini results provide you with sample data of your final results. It is a good idea for you to try the analysis you have planned for to make sure you know how it will turn out.

Doing the analysis based on a pilot study will pave the way for your final results. You may build your data sheet in an analysis software application such as SPSS or Nvivo. This same preparation will be used later on. This process may give you hints to modify the final methodology to better suit the following analysis stage.

For example, you may find out that the data you collected have open ended questions that can be multiple-choice questions. This change will help you a lot with the analysis later in the process. You may also find out that you missed an important question that can enhance the validity of the survey sample. Let's say you forgot to ask if the respondent is over 18 years old. How can you make sure to remove those who are not 18 years old from the final responses? By having a question in the survey that identifies the participant's age.

Validity and reliability are major foundations for the entire study. If your methodology has been proven invalid or unreliable, then your entire study is meaningless. Pilot studies help in achieving reliability and validity.

Reliability vs. Validity

Reliable	Low Validity	Not Reliable	Both Reliable
Not Valid	Low Reliablity	Not Valid	and Valid

Reliability means that if you conduct the study again, or someone duplicates your method, the same results are produced. In order to check for reliability, you need to use common sense. For example, if your study method has always been used for the same objective, then there is a good chance that your study method is reliable.

If your method has been tested in a pilot test, it means that you have checked that the method provides you with duplicable results. Making sure that every satisfied customer provides the same answer to the same question means that this question is reliable for measuring customer satisfaction. If a separate satisfied customer gives a different answer to the question, then it is not reliable in measuring customer satisfaction.

Reliability and validity have their own statistical tests if you are conducting quantitative research. These are mathematical calculations that will tell you the level of reliability and validity of your collected data. A Cranach's alpha test of 70% or higher is an example of internal consistency in your survey results. It makes sure that the data go together statistically.

If you want to test if a scale is reliable, you test it yourself several times in order to make sure it gives the same answer. If you test your weight on a scale, and every time you get a completely different answer, then you know the scale isn't reliable and you won't believe its results anymore.

Validity, on the other hand, is when you make sure that the method will generate the intended result. For example, if you try to measure your weight using a thermometer, you will not get your weight, but you will get a reliable temperature reading every time you use it. The point is, you have to use the proper tools. In this case, a scale. Not a thermometer.

Validity, similarly to reliability, requires common sense to ensure this method actually makes sense; that it generates the desired results. A pilot study helps achieve this objective. For example, before you use a thermometer to take the temperature of a sick person, you may want to use it on yourself first to ensure it works. Since you are not sick, you know that you should get a normal temperature. This process is a pilot test checking whether the thermometer is working. When you test the thermometer on more than one person at different times, you are checking the external validity of the measurement tool. When you make sure that the measurement is what you are supposed to be measuring, this is internal validity. But if you measure whether a patient has the flu, a thermometer is not enough. You also need to check the blood pressure as well as examine the throat and stomach of the patient. Therefore, you make sure that the measurement tool is measuring the entire construct. In this example, influenza. This is an example of construct validity. Influenza is a construct that cannot be measured by a single tool like the thermometer. Some people may do a face validity. Face validity is looking at the patient and determining whether he "looks like" a person with the flu. Face validity is a rather informal, subjective test and can be confirmed in your pilot study.

Some may claim that the existence of a certain type of bacteria predicts the existence of the flu. This is predictive validity.

Discriminate validity is conducted when checking for another type of bacteria that does not normally occur with the flu virus. Therefore, discriminate validity occurs when two measurements that seem to be unrelated are, in fact, unrelated.

There are more types of validity checks, and depending on your study, you may need to use more. Overall, a pilot study helps with the validity question. After you run a pilot study with your sample, you may ask them: do you think the survey measures my intended research question? This question covers the validity of your tool. The resulting discussion will help you fix any validity issues.

Survey vs. Interviews

Surveys are good to capture a wide range of answers by a large number of participants. These findings provide a chance to prove a point using many respondents who give evidence something is true. Therefore, one can generalize survey findings to the extent of the study.

On the other hand, interviews also get participant answers, but the power of interviews lies in the ability to ask in-depth questions. Interviews, whether face-to-face, by phone, or by online chats, provide much more information. They give the interviewer the chance to ask more questions and build on the discussion.

Surveys tend to be good when they have a limited number of answers that need to be confirmed, checked, or measured. As in quantitative research, the answers will be statistically processed. Interviews, on the other hand, are good to capture data that was not predictable by other means. Questions exploring a topic require a rich communication media to gather and process information to reach a conclusion in qualitative research. Questionnaires are type of surveys. The two terms can be used interchangeably. Even though some prefer to use questionnaires for pure statistical data gathering.

Sampling

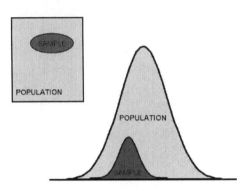

Your population includes all possible subjects of your study. If you are surveying oil companies in a geographical area, then all these companies will be your population. The population includes those you know, and those you do not know. The unit of analysis will be a company. A company is a legal entity that is being investigated by the study. If you were surveying purchasers of shampoo, then all people who purchase the shampoo are your population. The unit of analysis is a shampoo buyer.

Different studies will focus on different populations and samples. A case study will identify a specific population. The researcher of a case study focuses on a population of one organization, department, activity, process, etc. A quantitative study that needs to check if a theory applies to a population requires more focus on the population sample. A qualitative study may need to focus on a sample of the population that has answers to the exploratory questions. A phenomenological study would require a sample that includes particular traits.

What is your unit of analysis? Units of analysis can be employees, customers, students, patients, investors, workers, carpenters, sales people, organizations, IT firms, governmental organization, engineers, auditors, clinics, presidents, officers, creditors, advocates, legal cases, etc. It is important you understand what your population is, and what the unit under study is.

When you research a specific population, such as bank customers, you need to conduct your study on a sample from that population. The study sample provides a small set of the entire population and assumes that this sample represents the population. Once we understand the sample, then we can generalize the study and assume that what occurs in the sample occurs in the population under investigation.

The issue of generalizing study results to the population makes the sample very important. The sample has to provide, to an acceptable degree, a true representation of the population. Therefore, in your study you have to explain how your sample is representing the population. There are several sampling techniques that can produce reliable samples.

The best sampling technique is the random sampling. For example, assume you are surveying students at your university. You need to select a number of students who can represent the entire student body. In order to select a random sample, then you need to access the database and sort all students according to random numbers. Then select the required sample size.

There are many techniques on how to execute the random selection. There are random tables and there are Excel formulas that randomly sort a population. You just need to select them randomly.

Having a random sample means that every participant in the study has the same chance of being selected like everyone else. No student will have an advantage over anyone else to participate in the study. For example, a commuter will have the same chance as a student who lives on campus. Those who have more classes should have the same chance as those who have fewer classes. The elder will have the same chance as the younger, and so on.

The only way to get a random sample would be by having access to the student database. If your population includes all active students, Then you need to be able to select the active students from the database and exclude the non-active ones.

Once you have the random sample, then you need to approach these participants. Therefore, you need to have access to potential participants. You need to have their addresses or contact information. If you cannot reach them, then you may not be able to execute your study with this random sample.

What if you do not have access to the population database? In this case, you need to be creative in finding a way to reach a sample that is representative of your population. Using the *convenient sampling technique* is the easiest method. In convenient sampling, you just go to the cafeteria, or elsewhere on campus, and select the number needed for the sample size. You probably don't want to choose the mall to do convenient sampling for the active student-population; it is easier to go to campus.

Between random sampling and convenient sampling, there is a range of possible methods that can be used to assure the sample is representative of the population. For example, if you find out through school statistics that students are distributed equally among the university colleges, then you may want to make sure that your sample includes equal distribution among the colleges. If you know that there are certain demographic distributions in the student body, then you want to ensure each demographic is represented in your study. If you know that you have a certain percent of students who commute to the school, then you want a quota for the commuter population.

Generalization

The idea of making sure that your study is well represented makes your study findings generalized. If your sample is not representing the sample fairly, then the findings cannot be generalized to the entire population, but rather generalized to those who participated.

If your study is quantitative, you also need to address the issue of generalization. This is an important question for anyone who evaluates your study. If your sample effectively represents the population, then your study findings have a good chance of capturing the truth about your subject matter. This makes the examination of your study a valuable exercise. On the other hand, if your study sample is not a good representation of the population, then your findings are not necessarily true of the population.

The issue of generalization starts when you plan your methodology. Then, it is discussed in your findings. For example, if you use a random sample, or a quota sample, then you may want to compare the distribution of the sample responses with those of the population. This will be discussed in the descriptive analysis of the sample in your findings chapter. If none of the commuters responded to your study, then your study is limited to non-commuters. If a specific college is underrepresented in your study, then the findings may not accurately reflect that college.

If you do a case study, you will have in-depth findings of your case. Then you want to show how your case provides a sample that represents other similar organizations. This is a generalization issue.

If your study is a qualitative study, then you assume your findings are true for a wider population. The thesis or dissertation is a journey of finding the truth about the world. Therefore, as you find the truth, you have to describe how much of this truth is applicable to the world.

Sample size

Assume you want to check the taste of a tub of ice cream. A spoonful of the ice cream should be enough of a taste sample for the entire tub of ice cream. This is true given it is a homogeneous quantity of ice cream and you select a random spoonful.

If you have several tubs, then you may want to take one sample from each tub to make sure that each tub has the same taste. You can select a few random tubs from a large container of many tubs.

If you take three samples, and they all taste the same, that can be enough to generalize the taste over the entire population. Now if these three samples happened to taste differently, then your study cannot generalize anything. Your conclusion would say, try the research again. The research result has zero power to tell anything about the taste of the ice cream. This brings up the importance of power analysis in your survey findings. A researcher may decide to gather a larger sample to reduce the risk of reaching invalid or inconclusive results.

There are statistical techniques that can generate a suitable sample size depending on your type of analysis, the number of variables, the type of study, and other factors. You may look up suggested sample sizes for your type of study. If you are comparing two types of ice cream, then you have to have at least three samples from each pool in order to compare.

Data collection

Surveys

A survey is used to collect data from a large number of participants to reach a conclusion. Your survey can be online or offline. The findings will be further analyzed to reach a conclusion. Surveys operate as a measurement tool or a data collection device that will describe study variables.

Just like using a reliable thermometer to measure the temperature, you may want to use a good survey tool to measure your study variables. You can develop your own survey, but this may not be a reliable nor valid survey tool as discussed in the reliability and validity section.

Look up related research and see what survey tools are used to measure your variables. Use these tools for your study after proper permissions and citations. No need to re-invent the wheel if such surveys exist.

After you have your survey, you may want to do the pilot study as discussed previously. After you have your survey ready, then you need to administer survey data collection. Data collection can be offline or online.

Online Survey

You can make use of online survey applications that can help you setup your survey online. It is easier to have a mentor who has used a specific one to advise you if it fits your survey needs. You can do the exercise by yourself, but this can be time-consuming when you realize at the end that a specific question would not turn out the way you want it.

Once you have selected the survey application, you have to create the survey and test it. It is important to get your advisor's OK of the test so you do not get negative comments on the survey after execution.

You also need to get the output files of the survey application. These files can be analyzed immediately if planned well, and can be a nightmare if data was not coded correctly. A mentor on this item can make a huge difference. Some of these online applications have consultants. Reach out to them; they will save you lots of analytical work. They may even save you money that was originally budgeted to go to the statistician helping you with the analysis. Some of these online applications can automatically do some of the analysis for you if setup correctly.

Some online survey applications already include template surveys that are ready for use. If you are looking for an employee satisfaction survey, you may already find it there. However, be careful when using these templates. Some templates were developed for corporate use that may not serve your academic requirements.

Hand distributed Survey

A pen and paper survey can provide you with access to certain participants. If you administer such a survey, you may need to consider hiring assistants. These assistants can help you distribute the survey, assist participants, and collect survey results. They can also help you with encoding survey results into Excel for further processing.

Research assistants require training. They also need to sign a confidentiality agreement. The confidentiality agreement needs to follow your program requirements, terms, and conditions.

The training needed for the assistants may include the following: (a) Assistants need to first understand the nature of the study, its purpose and its objectives, (b) they should take the survey and answer the questions pretending they are part of the target group, (c) a brief explanation of the topic is important so they can answer participants basic questions, (d) participants may find it helpful to see your analysis based on their answers.

In the training session, it is good to have to-do and not-to-do lists. These should address issues of privacy, confidentiality, the type of questions that can be answered by an assistant, how to approach participants, where, when, and who. If you have a sampling technique, then emphasize how the sample should look.

The survey hardcopy needs to be managed by you. You want to make sure that the survey contains the minimum number of pages. You may use columns if you have many multiple-choice questions. Make sure to use a font that is easy-to-read and photocopy. Make sure that the survey photocopies are clear, since mass photocopying can generate poor quality photocopies.

When photocopying, I suggest that you use high-quality colored paper. Choose a color you like. The reason to use a quality colored paper is that it captures the participants' attention. It also acts as a reminder to finish the survey if the participant isn't done. It also stands out when collecting them, especially in offices where many papers may lay all over the place.

It can be helpful to write numbers on the surveys to be distributed. These numbers can be used to count the amount of returned surveys per assistant. For example, the first assistant will have surveys starting from 100; the second will have surveys starting from 200, and so on. This also motivates the assistants to reach their targets, if they know their work is identified. It may also help you during your analysis, if each assistant surveys a specific location. While this type of analysis will depend on your study objectives, it can help you during the reliability tests. You may find out that the survey distributed in a specific location produced outlier data that requires further analysis. I had a student who decided to drop all surveys collected by an assistant due to miscommunication that occurred during the survey collection process.

Mail Survey

If you decide to do a mail survey, you may be able to reach a variety of audiences in different locations who may meet your sampling requirement. The main problem with the survey is that it takes time due to a higher percentage of unreturned surveys.

To do an effective mail survey, you may want to include a pre-stamped envelope with your survey. You may also want to send a reminder for those who do not respond by the due date. Send a teaser post card before sending the survey announcing they have been selected to participate in an upcoming survey. Gift cards and other incentives may also work for you depending on your audience.

Phone survey

You may want to consider doing a phone survey, or more accurately a phone interview. Phone surveys take less time as you get immediate responses. You may want to hire assistants as discussed with the face-to-face survey administration. Phone surveys can reach participants who are geographically disbursed. In addition, a phone survey can give you a random sample in specific locations. Callers understand that not every random call is answered, but eventually, you will reach your required sample size.

A phone conversation gives the responder a chance to ask questions or ask for clarification that is not available in the mail survey.

Interview

Interviews are exploratory in nature. When you conduct an interview, you are exploring a specific topic. Therefore, you need to give the interviewee a chance to elaborate and think aloud about the topic. You want to ask open-ended questions and avoid any of your own preconceived conclusions about the topic. It is more difficult to hire assistants for an interview as they will require much training in the topic on order to do a good job.

Interviews need to be structured with predetermined questions that the interviewer is going to ask the interviewee. These questions guide the discussion and try to get an answer to the research study questions. Interviewers need to prepare the interview questions with the advisor and do research on the topic and the interviewee.

The number of interviews can be small, unlike the survey that requires a pool of participants. There can be 10 to 20 interviewees, depending on the topic. These interviewees will be selected based on a predetermined set of rules. The rules will depend on the objective of the study.

The interviewing journey looks for high-quality interviewees and their ability to bring a good and reliable description of the research phenomena. The exploration journey can achieve its objective from a few interviews. In summary, look for high-quality interviewees, and those who will enrich the topic.

When interviewing, you need to record the entire conversation, transcribe it, and analyze the findings. Several software programs will help you with this process such as Atlas, or Nvivo. These qualitative research tools can take audio files and transcribe them for you if the recordings are clear and the language is supported. The transcription of the interview will allow you to find common themes and reach conclusions.

Focus Groups

Instead of an interview, you may want to use a focus group of 4 to 10 participants. A focus group is another qualitative research method that gives you the chance to explore phenomena. A focus group is similar to an interview with many people at once. The benefit is that you can get more in depth findings.

As a group of homogeneous participants discusses a specific topic, participants contribute to underlying themes more effectively and efficiently. For example, if one says a problem mainly comes from employees and the other four participants disagree, then you have immediate feedback. On the other hand, if one says that the problem comes from customer understanding and everyone else supports the comment, and then you have an agreed finding. In addition, elaborating on the topic can dig deeper on what is it exactly that customers misunderstood.

When selecting the group, you need to make sure it is a homogeneous group, meaning all the participants have similar expertise about the subject and can build on each other's opinions. If you have incompetent or out of the context participants, you will not be able to dig deep in your research.

A focus group requires good planning. This includes selecting and managing a suitable time and place. When you start the session, you need to explain the study objectives, ask questions, get feedback from all the participants, be aware of the dominant few who control the discussion, give everyone a chance to express their views, observe the interactions, record the session, and maybe even have an assistant. A focus group assistant can help with recording, note taking, observing behavior, and moderation of the discussion. Two moderators can make sure that the focus group is on track.

Findings

Spend Time Analyzing

The analysis component is the part of your study that is most worth your time. Critical analysis can be time-consuming, but at the same time, it is a rewarding experience. The analysis will determine the significance of your study. Critical analysis produces an interesting study, and an interesting journey. Poor analysis produces frustration when writing your conclusions, and potentially meaningless recommendations. Therefore, arranging for good analysis requires doing a good job looking at the findings, analyzing them, and reporting them.

Critical analysis is achieved when you can put your findings in their broader context. It is when you can make a strong argument about your findings. An argument that is critical to the subject matter is one that everyone needs to know and pay attention to. A strong argument means that there are implications to these findings that may change the status quo. In other words, you provide a reason for academics and practitioners to change.

Check Your Findings Against Others

Your findings will need to be compared with other research in the same field. Your study probably has a base study that you used for development. Therefore, as you reach conclusions, you need to compare these findings with the broader community in your subject field. In the end, your research needs to be discussed by this community, so relating it to them provides an insight to how your contribution related to everyone else's.

Sample Description

Your findings will describe the results of your study. If you ran a survey, you would describe the sample surveyed. You will include a descriptive analysis of the sample.

For example, if you asked about the participant's gender, then you will report how many were male, and how many were female. If your population should be split fifty-fifty, male and female, and your sample happens to only include females, then here you will describe the sample, and provide analysis that this study was not limited to only female participants. If your sample proportion of females is only 25 per cent, then you may indicate that your sample under-represents females.

If you conducted an experiment, then here you will start to describe all the steps, and results of the study. You will describe and report these findings. The same thing applies if you did an interview; you will describe what every interviewee indicated in the interviews.

Statistical Methods

If your study is quantitative or an experiment, then you will probably need to provide statistical analysis of your findings. For example, if you study is a correlation study, you will need to conduct the correlation analysis and discuss whether they were significant or not.

If you have a proposed model, you may want to fit the data to the model and calculate the model fitness. If you are conducting statistical analysis, then you will need to conduct the statistical process, report the findings, and analyze them.

Descriptive statistics is the study of describing the basic statistics of the study. For example, you may want to report the averages, standard deviations, medians, etc. These descriptive statistics will describe the sample and provide an understanding of the survey question responses.

Inference statistics are used to examine the relationships between different variables. Most studies are interested in relationships between variables to reach a conclusion that describes world dynamics. These inferences indicate independent and dependent variable relationships. A moderate effect on a relationship is also an inference. Inference statistics is a major type of statistical analysis.

If you are not skilled in statistics, then you need to have access to a statistician. If you believe you know the basics, but you need an expert for the level of your thesis, then it would be better if you read about, and hired a tutor in statistics who can teach you what to do and at the same time confirm your steps, results, and conclusions. This is a chance for you to learn statistics. In the end, being a researcher means you know statistics.

If you want to learn about statistics, I would like to take you on this journey. This example has been well received by many students in understanding the concept of normal distribution. You probably have seen a bell curve before. A bell curve is a normal distribution.

Normal Distribution

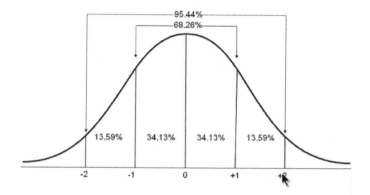

Figure 1: Normal Distribution

To understand the power of normal distribution, try this example. Get a pair of dice, throw them and write down the resulting two numbers. Repeat this process several times. After your write them down, add up the two numbers. Each of the dice will display a number between one and six. When you add up the two numbers, you will get a number between 2 and 12. If you look at the numbers generated, you can see that you will have lots of the number 7, and very few of the numbers 2 and 12.

When you roll the dice, there is a small probability both dice display the number 1 or 6, while there is a significant probability the value of both dice equals seven. The number 7 is generated if you roll the following combinations: (1 and 6), (2 and 5), (3 and 4), (4 and 3), (5 and 2), or (6 and 1). The chance of getting a total of 7 is obviously much higher than the chance of getting a 2 or 12. If you create a histogram of all the numbers, you will get the bell curve, or the normal distribution curve.

What is a histogram? A histogram is a chart that shows the frequencies of a possible outcome. In this example, the frequency of rolling 2 12 is low, and the frequency of rolling 7 is high. In the appendix, I provide a deeper explanation on how to construct a histogram.

Qualitative Studies

If you used an interview to collect your data, then you will probably get lots of text. This text can also be analyzed. While the quantitative methods can be accurately measured given we have knowledge in mathematics and statistics, qualitative methods have also been developed and now we have software that can measure qualitative data. Nvivo is software that can analyze text and find patterns and relationships in qualitative data.

For example, if you interview people about what is wrong with a specific issue, the transcription will show what interviewees mentioned as problems. Nvivo will identify similar problems and correlate them. Then you will be able to see all the themes or patterns among the interviewees. With researcher intervention, the software can search for particular themes in lots of text. It can also sort these themes based on categories, types of texts, participants, time, and many other qualitative or quantitative variables.

The interview results can generate tables, graphs, and numbers that can be statistically analyzed further. The objectives would be to find underling themes that can be further checked and verified.

For example, if you are seeking to understand why a new customer satisfaction program failed, the answers by selected interviewees can reach common themes such as the problem is with poor employee training, or customers did not understand the program, or the computer system was not helpful. These are three themes that the research found. The findings will include what each of the interviewees said about each of the three themes.

Using qualitative research software can actually help you quantify these themes, and prioritize the themes based on the proportion of people reporting them. It can also provide you with analysis such as how the views of female interviewees were different from male interviewees. While these themes can be reached simply with manual work, more complicated research questions can reach better conclusions with more sophisticated analysis.

Have you seen a tag cloud? If not, then search "word cloud." Alternatively, go to a website called worditout.com, then copy and paste the transcription of one interviewee. The result is a cloud of all the words in the transcription with different font sizes. The larger the font of the word, the more frequent this word was mentioned in the transcript. This shows how common themes float to the top when you analyze qualitative data. The qualitative research software will do that, but it also combines similar words that have the same meaning. It also links them with other variables.

Results

Ultimately, your results section should provide the answer to your research questions. It should include the test results of your hypothesis. You need to include a discussion on how your findings reflect the literature review in relation to your specific findings. The results section introduces the research project, illustrates the data collection process, reports the findings, describes these findings, analyzes them, and provides a level of significance to these findings.

Conclusions

Earn Your Degree Moments

There is a moment in your journey, when you will feel that you have transformed from the person who started the program to the person who earned his or her degree. Officially, you earn your degree when your thesis or dissertation is approved. Publicly, you earn your degree after you walk down the aisle at your graduation ceremony. However, you truly earn your degree at the moment when you realize that you have completed your study.

The moment you earn your degree is a special moment. You will likely be very tired, yet you will be enjoying the work on your thesis. That moment is for you to celebrate. It means you just have to finish the writing.

Answering Research Questions

Your conclusion should clearly answer the research questions. It should provide a good background picture of your problem, what research questions were asked, and what findings lead to your conclusion. This chapter can be written once. In fact, I advise you to write it all once so you have a complete conclusion to your study. If  you split it, you may start to repeat yourself, and start to bring outside topics into your conclusion.

Your written conclusion should be the culmination of your research journey. Some students are tempted to include conclusions not supported by the research findings. Therefore, the best way to do the conclusion is to follow the organization of your findings. Conclude every finding you have in Chapter 4. When writing your conclusion, keep in mind that professionals in your industry will only read your conclusion. Therefore, try to keep it simple, relative and to the point. You want to make sure your conclusions are supported by your data first, and then supported by the literature. Make sure to be precise about your conclusions as they reflect your findings. You do not want misinterpretations of your conclusions that your findings do not support.

Stay away from definitive statements. Show modesty in your findings that articulate the study limitations. For example, if you say in your conclusion, "This research study proves that…," then you are bragging about your study and asserting you have definitely proved your conclusions. This attitude may close doors for future research that may support your conclusions, and open doors to research showing your study had major limitations.

I remember Dr. Robert Johnson who acted as a committee member for my doctorate degree. He reminded me that people believed the sun orbited the earth for a long time and insisted they had proof, until Galileo came in and challenged this "fact."

In short, use the terms: "the findings of the study seem to indicate …", and those similar. This will give an indication that your findings also include limitations. You may have overwhelming support for your hypothesis, but your data is unlikely to prove it because future data set can always prove it wrong.

Providing Insights

Discussing the conclusions requires putting them in a larger context. You have to compare your findings to other research which should be discussed in your literature review. A link should exist between your survey of the literature in Chapter 2 and your conclusions in Chapter 5. If your findings agree or disagree with the literature, you will need to indicate that in your conclusion. If your conclusions agree with the literature, cite it to confirm the existing literature. If your findings contradict existing literature, clearly state this fact and provide insight why.

If your findings disagree with the literature, explain the disagreement. This explanation is either new knowledge, just like Galileo's discovery the earth orbits the sun. Alternatively, provide possible explanations for the unexpected results you discovered. In either case, you have something worth examining.

When the findings disagree with the literature, you may need to take another look at the literature and determine if there are findings within the literature that can help you explain your conclusions. As you dig more into the literature, you may find something worthy to be included in Chapter 2.

Recommendations

Your recommendations should also follow the same order and organization of your conclusions. You can provide a recommendation based on every conclusion you have reached. These conclusions can be divided into two sections. One for future researchers and one for practitioners. These recommendations also need to be based on your research findings, not based on your personal views on the topic.

Based on my experience with students, I see students come with recommendations their study can never reach. While qualitative research may reach recommendations that were unexpected, quantitative research is much more restricted. Even qualitative research can provide unexpected findings; the recommendation will be based on the conclusions that covered detailed findings in Chapter 4. Therefore, make sure that your recommendations come from your well-described findings.

Future Research

When advising future research, think about what you have learned and what you have concluded. If your research was qualitative, then you may want an examination of your conclusions via a survey. If your research was quantitative, you might recommend investigating the top and the bottom evaluations. Unexpected findings provide an opportunity to be discussed and included in your future research recommendation. Future research may also comment on your recommendation regarding study methodology and literature review.

Limitations

Remember the oath taken in a court of law, "I swear to say the truth, the whole truth, and nothing but the truth." Your limitations section gives you the chance to identify any shortcomings in your study. The limitations section is confirmation by the author that he or she knows about a shortcoming in the research process the reader needs to know about before generalizing the study.

The study limitations may include any concerns you had with the final thesis or dissertation. It may include any flaws or weaknesses. If you could not include an important section of your study, you list it here. You may need to justify past actions or intentions to help the reader understand your logic.

Any challenges you face are part of the limitations. If your data turns out to be unreliable, then you just say that in your limitations section. Other limitations may include a bad sample, very small sample size, or invalid literature.

Delimitations are associated with your limitations. For example, a limitation can be a very short time for conducting a survey. The delimitation would be your inability to reach those who do not use computers.

Assumptions

Part of affirming the whole truth is spelling out your assumptions. Your assumptions are the underlying beliefs you held while doing the research. For example, it is an assumption that you believe your sample is a good representation of the population. If you decide to not search for your lost key in a particular place, then you are assuming it is not there. This assumption needs to be spelled out.

Economic models tend to include many assumptions. For example, as prices go down, people buy more. There is an underling assumption that everything else is held constant.

Appendixes

Theses and dissertations may include appendixes that include additional information that operates as an integral component of the research study. You may include your data collection instrument such as interview questions, permissions to use copyrighted materials included in your study, signed confidentiality agreements, and tables and graphs that a reader may need to look up for further analysis.

DEFENSE

You have finished your thesis. Your advisor is happy with it. Your committee may or may not have approved it depending on your program. Now, you have to stand up in front of everyone else. They are people you might or might not have known before the defense. Your task is to show what you have done. Your task is to provide evidence that you are an expert in the thesis or dissertation topic. You did it, not someone else. As a result, you can handle any question in this field of study. You will be able to discuss every part of it and show you knew what you were doing. The objective of the defense is to prove you are an expert in your thesis topic.

How do you prepare for the defense? You need to prepare a short presentation that will be discussed in the following section. This presentation needs to be easy, clear, understandable, and short. Make sure you get to the point that highlights your research journey. It should provide evidence that you know the topic well, and you can smoothly explain what you did in your research. You also need to be able to discuss the findings and conclusions. More importantly, you should be able to answer questions from the committee.

What will the committee ask you in your defense? Many questions can come up in your defense. The best way to prepare for it is to make a good thesis at the beginning. If you do not know what you are doing, then it is difficult or impossible to prepare for the defense. However, most programs and advisors will not let that happen.

If you break the questions into categories, they will be as follows:

- Technical Questions: These will be issues with your thesis writing style, formatting, numbering, tables, figures, missing pages, authors, or paragraphs.

- Literature Questions: "Did you check the findings of Author X?" This is a very difficult question if you if you've excluded the research of a key player in your research topic. You cannot talk credibly about certain topics without knowing its key contributors. Make sure to follow your model journal article and its references.

- Methodology Questions: These questions check your measurement tool reliability. Did your survey measure the different variables effectively? It can also include questions about sample issues including size, selection, representation, pilot study, participants, etc. Make sure you understand your methodology, and why you used it.

- Analysis Questions: "You mentioned 'X', but why is that a factor?" These questions occur when you focus too much on the trees and you miss the forest. If your analysis is too long, and you repeat it too much, you will fall into this trap. Keep your analysis short, simple, and to the point. Nothing else.

- Conclusions Questions: "So if you were in this position, what would you do?" This can be a tricky question, since the position described can be a real application of your study, yet the correct answer should come from your conclusions. It would be funny if you recommend doing things differently from what you suggested in your thesis.

- Generalization Questions: It is important your study generalization is explained in your defense, and will likely be challenged if you say it is generalizable.

- Limitations Questions: Any weakness in your study becomes a limitation in the study. You have to be brave to show and discuss your study weaknesses. At the moment, you may feel that you did a poor job, but it is OK. In fact, it is purely normal. It is just an exercise.

- Reality Questions: Questions that have nothing to do with your research but rather has to do with the field of study in general. The person who asks you this question probably has some knowledge about the topic, and wants to get your opinion.

What is the best answer during the defense? "That is a very important point. I will reflect it in my study." During the defense, you will likely hear several common comments. For example, "This does not make sense." "This needs to be changed." "This is not accurate." "This is not correct." In each of these cases, you may clarify your opinion. Nevertheless, if you clarify your opinion once, and the other party does not buy it, then it is safe for you to say, "I will investigate and fix my thesis if necessary."

During the defense, the committee wants you to graduate but before that, they want you to learn a bit more and the defense is their last chance to help you learn before you graduate. So give them that chance. Thank them for their contributions and help given since the beginning of the program.

When do people fail during the defense? The main reason is your failure to get your advisor's OK. The committee may argue the advisor should fail you if you have misled him or her. The only reason you could fail that I can think of is an ethical violation. You just have to follow the rules.

Presentation

During your defense, you may be able to use a power point presentation to go over your thesis or dissertation. The program may already have a template that students ought to use for their presentation. If so, the template should include parts required by the program. Just fill it in.

It is suggested to keep the presentation short. Use short sentences, or just keywords that remind you of what you will be talking about. You should sound like an expert in your presentation. You are expected to have memorized the name of the author of your model journal article. You should know the theory you are basing your study on inside out. You have memorized some of the key findings of your study. This is because you have spent a good time studying them.

Some of the facts you want to mention in your presentation include the reason for selecting the topic. What makes this topic relevant to you on a personal level? What surprised you during your research process? What findings did you not expect that emerged and what does it mean? Did that affect your research study?

Your responses should be short and in relation to your study. Do not overdo it. What you should overdo though are your methodology and data collection. At least half of your presentation should be discussing your work, not anyone else's.

Based on most common presentation templates, you will have to do an introduction to your thesis, where you will tell the audience what is going to be covered in your presentation. Then you will provide background on your topic and conclude it with your problem statement. Next, you will need to discuss why your problem statement is important. Then you will provide the research questions. After that, you can talk about what others have done to answer these questions. Do not repeat your literature review. Just briefly highlight a few. Then get into what you did. As you discuss your methodology, your tools, and your techniques, you can also refer to the relevant literature review.

What you did in the research project is the most important part of your presentation. The audience wants to make sure that it is your work, and you understand what you did. The presentation should prove that well. [16]

As you discuss your methodology, you will provide your findings and conclusions. In addition, you probably are going to include references from the literature. Do not worry if you go back and forth between the chapters. The objective is to show all of your work during your presentation time.

It is always good to have figures or graphs that contain a lot of information on one screen. It also serves well during the defense to have your findings on one slide. If you have lots of information, consider printing it and hanging it on flip charts for easy reference.

Using flip charts offers a communication advantage during your defense. If your topic includes many similar components such as an analysis that generates different results, and the audience may be confused by which data belongs to which analysis, you may want to put each analysis on a separate flip chart. Therefore, they can point to the analysis they will discuss with you.

You may consider having every slide on a large piece of paper posted on the wall in order of your presentation. So, if someone asks you a question, you stand next to that post and discuss it. It also allows you to write on that slide, which may put an end to a comment brought by the committee. This also reduces confusion when you have to find a specific slide during the discussion.

Part of your presentation is to prepare for the defense. It is advisable to attend one before it's your turn. Ask your advisor or your program coordinator how to attend a defense. It will motivate you and will provide valuable experience on what could be asked during yours. There are frequently asked questions during defense and they can be even more specific in your program. Different programs have a strategic plan for their program quality. Therefore, if you ask those before you about their experiences, there is a good chance you will get very similar, if not exactly the same common questions.

After your defense, you can celebrate with your family and friends. However, it is probably not the end of the journey. Sometimes, you are still not entitled to the degree. There is a good chance you will still have to address the comments by your committee. You will probably still have to consult with your advisor to see if you have fixed them properly, and contact the committee to approve you for the degree.

Publication

You have not yet finished. This is the best time to publish your work. Even if you believe it was just a journey in the beginning, you probably have evolved. Now, you are a different creature. You have earned your degree, and now your work can be published in the best journals. You just have to go the extra mile to make it available to the world.

Your advisor will be there to help you. If your advisor is not interested, some other advisor or committee member may be interested in co-authoring your research. If you do not do it now, you will probably never do it. It will help your career, and it is your right. Just as it is your right to get your degree, it is also your right to get your work published.

REFERENCES

1.   Boote, D. N. & Beile, P. Scholars Before Researchers: On the Centrality of the Dissertation Literature Review in Research Preparation. *Educ. Res.***34,** 3–15 (2005).

2.   Mullins, G. & Kiley, M. Mullins 2002 PhD examiners assess. *Stud. High. Educ.***27,** 369–386 (2002).

3.   Clark, I. L. *Writing the Successful Thesis and Dissertation: Entering the Conversation.* (Prentice Hall Press, 2006). doi:0-13-173533-0

4.   Ridley, D. *The literature review: a step-by-step guide for students.* (Sage, 2008). at <http://www.amazon.com/The-Literature-Review-Step-Step/dp/1412934257>

5.   Creswell, J. W. *Research Design: Qualitative, Quantitative, and Mixed Methods Approaches.* (Sage publications, 1994). doi:http://dx.doi.org/10.1016/j.math.2010.09.003

6.   Madsen, D. Successful dissertations and theses: a guide to graduate student research from proposal to completion. 244 (1992). at <http://books.google.ps/books?id=wDgQAQAAMAAJ>

7.   Punch, K. F. *Developing Effective Research Proposals.* (Sage, 2000). doi:9780585386072

8.   Delamont, S., Atkinson, P. & Parry, O. *Supervising the Doctorate 2nd Edition.* (McGraw-Hill Education (UK), 2004).

9.   Eley, A. & Jennings, R. *Effective Postgraduate Supervision: Improving the Student/Supervisor Relationship.* (McGraw-Hill Education (UK), 2005).

10.   American Psychological Association (APA). *Publication manual of the American Psychological Association.* (Author, 2008).

11.   Easterby-Smith, M. *Management research.* (Sage, 2011).

12.   Blaikie, N. *Designing Social Research.* (Polity, 2000).

13.   Glaser, K. Deductive or Inductive?

14.   Kushkowski, J. D., Parsons, K. a. & Wiese, W. H. Master's and Doctoral Thesis Citations: Analysis and Trends of a Longitudinal Study. *portal Libr. Acad.***3,** 459–479 (2003).

15.   Piantanida, M. [Main author] & Garman, N. B. *The qualitative dissertation : a guide for students and faculty.* (Corwin Press, 2009).

16.   Roberts, C. M. *The dissertation journey : a practical and comprehensive guide to planning, writing, and defending your dissertation.* (Corwin Press, 2010). at <http://search.library.duke.edu/search?id=DUKE004654674>

APPENDIX A: HISTOGRAM

Histogram

Let us do a frequencies table and a histogram on excel as an exercise.

Open excel, and go to the first cell A1, and type this equation =int(rand()*6)+1. This equation will be similar to throwing a dice. It will generate a number between 1 and 6. The function rand() will generate a random number, while the int() function will make it an integer, and the +1 will make it start from 1, and the multiplication by 6 will make it reach up to 6.

Copy this function to the next column B. In column C, type = A1+B2. This will add up the two numbers. Then copy the three cells from the first row to row 100 or even 1000. Each row will be a throw of two dices and add them up.

Now we need to create the frequencies bin, which is the X-axis on the histogram chart. Go to cell E1 and type Bin, and in F1 type Frequencies. In cell E2 to E13 type the numbers 1to 12. Then highlight cells F2:F13, and type =FREQUENCY($C:$C,$E$2:$E$13) and then press ctrl+shift+Enter. This will generate the frequencies of all the summed pairs from column C. After that, highlight cells E1:F13 and click on insert scatter chart that will generate the bell curve.

If you press F9 on your Excel, then the random function will update and you will get new numbers. You see that the curve may slightly change depending on how many rows you have. The more rows, the more stable your curve remains.

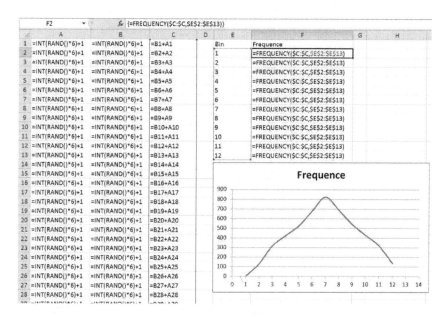

Figure 2: Throwing dices frequencies and histogram

If you need help on this exercise, try to look up "How to Use the FREQUENCY Function in Excel" on YouTube.

The conclusion of this curve is that while the process was completely random, we still can get a very good description of what the numbers will turn out to be if you add two numbers of two dices. This is the basic principle in the study of statistics. You can conclude that there is a 50% chance that the sum of the two dices will get you 7 or more. In addition, the chance of getting 1 is zero. If we look at the distribution, we can say that we are confident 100% that the sum of the two dices will be more than 1. We will conclude that it is impossible to get 1 as the sum of the two dices. While this is intuitive in this example, in your research study, you may want to use the same logic to reach the same conclusion.

In the dices example, the average of 7 is also called the mean. You can also measure the standard deviation, which will be around 2.4. Excel will calculate it for you, you type in the function

=stdev(C:C). This number means that if you take an average of 7, the deviation from that average would be 2.4 more or less. Therefore, you can be 68% confident that your sum of the two dices will be between 4.6 and 9.4 (7± 2.4).This 68% is fixed based on previous studies of the normal curve. This number also appears in Figure 1. If you take two standard deviations from the center then you will get the range 2.2 to 11.8. Meaning that 95% of your results will be within this range. It also says that there is only a 5% chance that you will get outside this range.

If you think about your survey questions, we are trying to get the histogram and then start to look at the middle answer that constitutes the average response. You will have few on the sides. These few and that middle is the results of the study. If you measure the time students arrive for the class, you can calculate the mean and standard deviation. If you measure it for different instructors, then you may also get the same mean and standard deviation. If you find a specific class that has a significant difference between its mean and all other classes, then you may have statistical evidence that this class is different. This can be an interesting finding to see what is happening in that class that can create a significant difference. This significant difference would mean that there is a reason other than randomness that creates the difference. Here is when you need to do the T test. When you compare the two curves of the normal classes, and the special class, then you will find that the two curves are separated.

If you ran an experiment to check the effectiveness of medication on a patient. You would measure the average and standard deviation of the blood pressure before, and after. Then you would run the T test. The T test would indicate that there is a significant difference between the two averages, meaning that medication in fact has altered the results. The probability that the change in the blood pressure is random has been eliminated, leaving the chance for the medication to be the only reason for the change in the blood pressure. Of course, you need to hold everything constant, so you eliminate any other possible cause of a high blood pressure. Maybe you want to run this experiment to several people who have the same health conditions to be able to see this is generalized at the power level.

Depending on your level of statistics, you may need to read more on statistics to fully understand these topics. Students who run statistical tests are expected to understand what they did. Some may say that students do not have to run the statistical procedures, but they should know what they mean.

Different statisticians can also look at the same problem and conduct several analyses based on the same data, you want to make sure to use the one that will help you finish your research. The findings can be very interesting and may expand the scope of your entire thesis, but this is not the time for such discoveries. Make sure to address the research minimum requirement to finish your study.

Many advanced methods would require advanced analysis. Unless you have to do it, it is better to remove it. I have seen many students stuck with their analysis, and at the end, I just suggest removing it all, and advising them to stick to the main analysis needed for the study.

Note that statistical procedures may have assumptions that need to be tested. For example, you may need to do a reliability test for the survey before you run a correlation. Then you may need to do a normality test before you run a correlation. A regression analysis may require no correlation between the variables. Therefore, as you start to use complicated methods, you need to be aware of what they mean and how they should be interpreted. So keeping it simple can ease your journey while achieving your objective to get your degree.

APPENDIX B: THESIS TOOLS

- Turn It In Report: Before you submit your final thesis, you may want to check it on http://turnitin.com/

- Install Mendeley with its word plugin to manage your references.

- Download a word thesis template from your program, or find one and customize it for your requirement.

- Search Google Scholar for your model research article, this will be your passport.

- Decide on your survey research instrument, this will be your ticket to triumph.

- Make use of MS Word navigation panel, learn how to use styles headings.

- Check with your university about your access to reputable journals, and limit your literature review to journal articles.

JOIN THE DISCUSSION

For more information about how to proceed with your thesis, please join http://thesis.tips/ , share your thoughts with your fellow new researchers and assist new students.

ABOUT THE AUTHOR

Dr. Alkibsi is the kind of professor most of us never had but wished we did. He is excited about having a meaningful long-term impact on the lives of his students. As an Associate Professor of Business Administration at Lebanese International University, he has assisted many students with writing their theses and dissertations.

Dr. Alkibsi's mission in education is to promote sound practices that can create benefit and establish value in the lives of others. He earned his BS and MBA from Murray State University in Murray, Kentucky. He completed his doctorate in business administration from the University of Phoenix.

As a university educator, he can shape the lives of future leaders and takes that responsibility very personally. His book, A Novice Guide to How to Write a Thesis, is a natural extension of that passion. Read more at http://sharaf.alkibsi.com/

About the book

This book is most useful to students looking forward to writing their thesis or dissertation. Advisors may recommend this book for their students at the early stage of their research project or if they struggle at any stage. The book addresses the big picture of the research journey, and provides advice on how to manage the entire process.

I have seen excellent students get stuck. All they needed to triumph was a piece of advice. I decided to write this book hoping to solve this problem for future students. Many small tips will be eye opening. A few tips will be mind blowing en route to scoring an outstanding thesis.

Made in the USA
San Bernardino, CA
09 April 2019